Caravan & Camping Holidays

in Britain

Holiday Parks & Centres

Caravan Sites & Touring Parks

Camping Sites

Caravans for Hire

Carnmoggas Holiday Park
St Austell, Cornwall

Castaways Holiday Park
Bacton-on-Sea, Norfolk

2013

www.holidayguides.com

Accommodation Standards: Star Grading Scheme

The AA, VisitBritain, VisitScotland, and the VisitWales now use a single method of assessing and rating serviced accommodation. Irrespective of which organisation inspects an establishment the rating awarded will be the same, using a common set of standards, giving a clear guide of what to expect.   They have full details of the grading system on their websites.

www.enjoyEngland.com

www.visitScotland.com

www.visitWales.com

www.theaa.com

Using a scale of 1-5 stars the objective quality ratings give a clear indication of accommodation standard, cleanliness, ambience, hospitality, service and food.

This shows the full range of standards suitable for every budget and preference, and allows visitors to distinguish between the quality of accommodation and facilities on offer in different establishments.
All types of board and self-catering accommodation are covered, including hotels, B&Bs, holiday parks, campus accommodation, hostels, caravans and camping, and boats.

Gold and Silver awards are given to Hotels and Guest Accommodation that provide exceptional quality, especially in service and hospitality.

The more stars, the higher level of quality

★
acceptable quality; simple, practical, no frills

★★
good quality, well presented and well run

★★★
very good level of quality and comfort

★★★★
excellent standard throughout

★★★★★
exceptional quality, with a degree of luxury

National Accessible Scheme Logos for mobility impaired and older people

If you have particular mobility impairment. look out for the National Accessible Scheme. You can be confident of finding accommodation or attractions that meet your needs by looking for the following symbols.

Older and less mobile guests
If you have sufficient mobility to climb a flight of steps but would benefit from fixtures and fittings to aid balance.

Part-time wheelchair users
You have restricted walking ability or may need to use a wheelchair some of the time and can negotiate a maximum of 3 steps.

Independent wheelchair users
You are a wheelchair user and travel independently. Similar to the international logo for independent wheelchair users.

Assisted wheelchair users
You're a wheelchair user and travel with a friend or family member who helps you with everyday tasks.

Contents

©MAPS IN MINUTES™ (2011)
Contains Ordnance Survey data
©Crown Copyright and database right 2010

symbols

 Holiday Parks & Centres

 Caravans for Hire

 Caravan Sites and Touring Parks

 Camping Sites

Get closer to the **great outdoors** with Haven

There's lots to discover with a choice of 23 UK touring and camping holiday parks. From golden beaches to heated pools, sports activities and kids' clubs, there's so much to do and it's all included in your pitch price. And, there's an also exciting range of 'pay as you go' activities including fencing, archery and golf.

As well as all the fun, we've covered the essentials

- Pick of 6 pitch types - from basic grass to fully serviced hard-standing
- We welcome tourers, motorhomes, tents and trailer tents
- Modern shower blocks and amenities
- 24-hour security with touring wardens on many parks
- Beach access on or near all parks
- Pets welcome for only £1* a night

Save up to
50%*
on 2013 holidays

To find out more, order a brochure and to book

Call: **0843 308 7818** Quote: TO_FHG13

Calls cost 5p per minute plus network extras. Open 7 days a week, 9am-9pm

Visit: **haventouring.com/tofhg13**

Haven touring +camping
Britain's Favourite Seaside Holiday

Cornwall

Bodmin

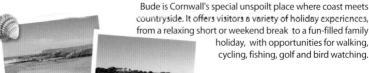

Bude

A unique Cornish 4 star holiday experience

Set in 55 acres of rolling countryside well away from the road and with stunning views of Looe Island and the sea beyond Tregoad Park offers the ideal location for both fun filled family holidays and quiet relaxing out of season breaks. Close to the pretty fishing town of Looe and beaches we can guarantee you a beautiful location, all the facilities and a very warm and friendly welcome.

We have 190 large flat & terraced pitches of which 60 are hardstanding ideal for touring caravans, motorhomes and tents. Most are southerly facing and all pitches have electric hook-up.

There are ample water and waste points around the park and access roads are tarmac so getting on and off your pitch is easy.

The toilet and shower facilities are modern, clean and free of charge and there is a launderette at the lower block. The reception building contains a well stocked shop and visitor information centre together with internet access point and post box.

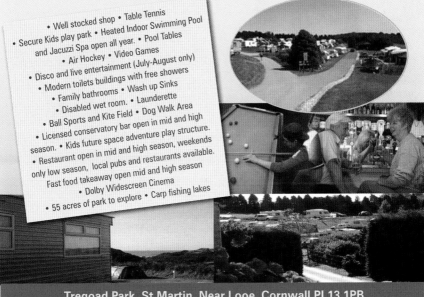

- Well stocked shop • Table Tennis
- Secure Kids play park • Heated Indoor Swimming Pool and Jacuzzi Spa open all year. • Pool Tables
- Air Hockey • Video Games
- Disco and live entertainment (July-August only)
- Modern toilets buildings with free showers
- Family bathrooms • Wash up Sinks
- Disabled wet room. • Launderette
- Ball Sports and Kite Field • Dog Walk Area
- Licensed conservatory bar open in mid and high season. • Kids future space adventure play structure.
- Restaurant open in mid and high season, weekends only low season, local pubs and restaurants available. Fast food takeaway open mid and high season
- Dolby Widescreen Cinema
- 55 acres of park to explore • Carp fishing lakes

Looe, Mevagissey

Trelay Farm Park

A small, peaceful, friendly, family-run site. It is quiet, uncommercialised and surrounded by farmland. The park lies on a gentle south-facing slope offering wide views of open countryside. Excellent new facilities include hot showers/launderette and disabled suite with wheelchair access. The three-acre camping field is licensed for 66 tourers/tents etc. Good access, generous pitches, hook ups. In adjoining area (1.5 acres) are 35 holiday caravans in a garden-like setting. The nearby village of Pelynt has shops, Post Office, restaurants, pub. Looe and Polperro are both just three miles away. The renowned Eden Project is 12 miles west. Luxury caravans for sale and rental. Pets welcome. Children's Play Area.

Pelynt, Looe PL13 2JX
Tel: 01503 220 900
e-mail: stay@trelay.co.uk
www.trelay.co.uk

CARNMOGGAS HOLIDAY PARK

A small, family-run, pet-friendly caravan park situated on the south coast of Cornwall, near Mevagissey, open all year round and ideally placed for seaside, country and town. Facilities include clubhouse with bar, indoor swimming pool, outdoor play area and three indoor bowling rinks. Close to many sandy beaches, Lost Gardens of Heligan, Eden Project, and picturesque fishing villages. Local amenities include golf, horse riding, mackerel and shark fishing, water sports and a Recreation Centre offering a range of sporting activities.

2010 and 2012 two/three bed caravans.
June Breaks from £125. July from £150

Carnmoggas Holiday Park
Little Polgooth, St Austell,
Cornwall PL26 7DD
Tel: 01726 74070 • e-mail: reception@carnmoggas.com • www.carnmoggas.com

symbols

 Holiday Parks & Centres

 Caravans for Hire

 Caravan Sites and Touring Parks

 Camping Sites

Marver Holiday Park

Mawgan Porth,
Near Newquay TR8 4BB

Small, quiet family-run site, offering beautiful views of the Lanherne Valley. Approximately 150 yards from the beach, which is excellent for children, surfers and fishing.
Only five miles from Newquay and eight miles from the historic fishing port of Padstow.

The site offers chalets and static caravans for hire and a level campsite suitable for caravans, motor homes and tents.

On site there is a toilet and shower block, sauna and launderette, in which there is a payphone, washing up facilities and a freezer for the use of our guests.

Nearby fishing, surfing, horse riding, golf and shops, also good public houses, surf board and wet suit hire.

Tel: 01637 860493
e-mail: familyholidays@aol.com
www.marverholidaypark.co.uk

Newquay

A park for all seasons

Trethiggey Touring Park

Quintrell Downs, Newquay TR8 4QR

Our friendly, family-run park is just minutes by car from Newquay's famous surf beaches and 15 miles from the amazing Eden Project. Beautifully landscaped, the park has panoramic countryside views and is ideal for touring caravans, tents and campervans.

We also have luxury holiday homes for hire. Facilities include shop, off-licence, free showers, electric hook-ups, laundry, children's play area, TV/games room, fishing, cafe, licensed bar, Bistro, take-away food in summer.

Open from March 1st to January 1st including Christmas and New Year. Short Breaks available. Off-season rallies welcome.

For more information phone
01637 877672
or see our website:
www.Trethiggey.co.uk
e-mail: enquiries@trethiggey.co.uk

Newquay, Padstow, Penzance

Perran Quay Touring Park • Newquay

A very friendly, family-run campsite on an elevated position overlooking the countryside and coast, all pitches are on straight and level ground. Every tent and caravan has its own pitch inc. parking space, and most have an electric hook up. There are several water stations and a chemical disposal point situated centrally. Showers. Launderette. Heated outdoor pool, children's padding pool and adventure playground. Static Caravans for hire. Local Bar and Restaurant.

Perran Quay Touring Park, Hendra Croft, Rejerrah TR8 5QP
Tel. 01872 572561 • e-mail: rose@perran-quay.co.uk • www.perran-quay.co.uk

Trevean Farm

St Merryn, Padstow PL28 8PR

Small, pleasant site close to several sandy beaches with good surfing and lovely, golden sands. Splendid sea views. Golf club within 2 miles. Village shops one mile. Sea and river fishing nearby. Three static six-berth luxury caravans with cooker, fridge, mains water supply, flush toilet, shower and digital TV. Modern toilet/shower block with free showers. Family room with disabled facilities. Electric hook-ups. Pay phone, children's play area and small shop (Whitsun to September) on-site. Wi-Fi available. Pets permitted in tents and tourers but not in static caravans. Weekly rates for static vans from £200 to £480 according to season. Touring caravans and tents welcome from £8 to £12 per night. Open Easter to October.

Tel: 01841 520772 • e-mail: trevean.info@virgin.net

Old MacDonald's Farm and Campsite
Padstow • Cornwall

A small, family-run farm park and campsite just half a mile from the North Cornish coast between Padstow and Newquay. Ideal base for touring this magnificent Area of Outstanding Natural Beauty, the perfect choice for families, walkers or anyone just wanting a quiet relaxing break.
50 good size pitches, 20 with electric hook-up. 6 shower rooms, additional toilets, laundry and washing up facilities. Free use of farm park facilities. Café and small games room on site.

John and Karen Nederpel, Old MacDonald's Farm, Porthcothan Bay, Padstow, Cornwall PL28 8LW
Tel. 01841 540829 • enquiries@oldmacdonalds.co.uk • www.oldmacdonalds.co.uk

Tower Park is a peaceful, family-run campsite ideally situated for stunning beaches, the coastal path and the Minack Theatre. We offer large, level pitches for tents and tourers and static holiday caravans for hire and are just a five minute level walk from St Buryan village with its pub, shop and Post Office.

Tower Park Caravans & Camping
St Buryan, Penzance TR19 6BZ
01736 810286

e-mail: enquiries@towerparkcamping.co.uk • www.towerparkcamping.co.uk

Wheal Rose
Caravan & Camping Park

A secluded, 6-acre family-run touring park, central for all West Cornwall. Adjacent to the park is Mineral Tramway popular with walkers and cyclists. The park consists of 50 level, grassed pitches with electrical hook-ups. Spotlessly clean, purpose-built shower/toilet block, shop, children's play area, TV/games room, laundry and disabled facilities.

HEATED OPEN AIR SWIMMING POOL

Prices from £12.00 per night. Open March to December.

Scorrier, Redruth TR16 5DD
Tel/Fax: 01209 891496

e-mail: les@whealrosecaravanpark.co.uk
www.whealrosecaravanpark.co.uk

St Agnes, Truro

Summer Valley Touring Park

Shortlanesend, Truro TR4 9DW

Situated just two miles from Truro, Cornwall's cathedral city, and ideally placed as a centre for touring all parts of Cornwall. This quiet, small, secluded site is only one-and-a-half miles from the main A30 and its central situation is advantageous for North Cornwall's beautiful surfing beaches and rugged Atlantic coast or Falmouth's quieter and placid fishing coves. Horse riding, fishing and golf are all available within easy distance. This compact site is personally supervised by the owners. Facilities include a toilet block with free hot water, washing cubicles, showers, shaving points, launderette, iron, hairdryer, etc; caravan electric hook-ups; children's play area. Shop with dairy products, groceries, bread, confectionery, toys, Calor/Camping gas.

Two people, car, caravan/tent £12 to £16 per day

Mr and Mrs J.S. Findlay
Tel: 01872 277878 • www.summervalley.co.uk

Truro

Trevarth
Holiday Park . Cornwall

Trevarth is a small, well-kept family-run park excellently situated
for north and south coast resorts.
All our luxury caravan holiday homes are modern with all main services.
Tourers and campers are well catered for with level pitches,
some sheltered, with ample hook-ups.

- A quiet caravan and camping park, offering a friendly
and personal service, with over 30 years' experience.
- Caravans set amongst beautifully kept, peaceful and mature gardens.
- Well maintained and level touring and camping fields,
with electric and some hard standings
- No noisy nightclub or bar.
- Children's play area and games room.
- Situated in the centre of Cornwall making our
holiday park an ideal base to further explore Cornwall

ROSE AWARD
CARAVAN HOLIDAY PARK
2011

AA
▶▶▶▶
🚐 🚐 ⛺

enjoyEngland.com
★★★★
HOLIDAY, TOURING
& CAMPING PARK

Blackwater, Truro TR4 8FR
e-mail: trevarth@btconnect.com
www.trevarth.co.uk
Tel: 01872 560266
Fax: 01872 560379

Gunvenna Holiday Park

Gunvenna Holiday Park is a well-drained site of level grassland on 10 acres commanding uninterrupted views of the countryside within five minutes' drive of safe golden sandy beaches.
It makes the ideal holiday park for families and couples.

There are large spacious pitches some of which are fully serviced; mains water, gray waste, and electric.

If you are looking to spend your holiday in a relaxing part of the south west of England this area will not disappoint.

Local activities include golf, fishing, tennis and cycle hire. Visit the Eden Project or go karting at St Eval Kart Circuit.

St Minver, Wadebridge PL27 6QN
Tel: 01208 862405 • www.chycor.co.uk/gunvenna

• Touring caravan electric hook-ups 16 amp.
• A modern toilet and shower block with FREE hot and cold water shaving points and hairdryers. • Guests disabled toilet. • Launderette. • Post box.
• Ample mains water points. • Chemical disposal units.
• Waste water drains. • Children's play area on sand.
• Games room. • Telephone kiosk (outgoing only).
• Dog exercise area and shower. • On site shop. • Indoor heated swimming pool.

AA

2002

The Camping and Caravanning Club
The Friendly Club

Devon

Branscombe

Visit the FHG website
www.holidayguides.com
for all kinds of holiday accommodation in Britain

Our Unforgettable view... **Galmpton Touring Park**

Galmpton Touring Park is an award winning family park in a stunning location catering exclusively for touring caravans, tents and motorhomes. Our two separate caravan and camping fields enjoy spectacular views over the broadest reaches of the River Dart.
Excellent toilet/shower facilities, including disabled and Under-5's bathroom. Dishwashing and laundry. As well as electric hook-ups we offer some deluxe pitches with electric hook-up, water connection and sink waste drain.
Surrounded by countryside, we are a short walk away from the local village shops and a pub which serves good food. There is plenty nearby for adults and children alike.
Special off-peak reductions.
We only accept families and couples. Sorry no dogs in main season
We also have two holiday apartments.

Galmpton Touring Park, Greenway Road,
Brixham,Devon TQ5 0EP • Tel: 01803 842066 enquiries@galmptontouringpark.co.uk
www.galmptontouringpark.co.uk

Chudleigh, Devon TQ13 0DZ
Tel: 01626 853785
Email: enquiries@holmanswood.co.uk
Web: www.holmanswood.co.uk

A warm welcome awaits you at our delightful personally managed Holiday Park in this picturesque part of Devon.
Neat and attractive, easy access from the A38. Gateway to Dartmoor.
Close to Haldon Forest - Exeter - Newton Abbot- Torquay.
Sandy beaches at Dawlish and Teignmouth.

Club **Wi Fi**

★ Touring / Seasonal Pitches
★ Holiday Homes for Sale
★ Summer & Winter Storage
★ Tents welcome in our 8 acre Meadow
★ Excellent Toilets / Showers
★ Launderette / Washing up area / WiFi

192/24

St John's Farm

Caravan & Camping Park

St Johns Road, Withycombe, Exmouth Devon EX8 5EG

Our unique situation away from the hustle and bustle of the main town of Exmouth is ideal for those seeking a little peace and quiet, yet is ideally situated as a base to explore all the things that Devon is famous for, including Orcombe Point, the start of the East Devon Heritage Coast.

The caravan park and camp site is situated in pleasant pasture land with rural views, yet only 10 minutes away from two miles of glorious sandy beaches or unspoilt heathland.

Stop overnight, spend a weekend with us, or stay for a month! Whatever you choose you will be assured of a warm Devonshire welcome at this family-run site.

Facilities include:

- Electric hook-ups
- Toilets / Disabled facilities
- Hot and cold showers / hair drying facility
- Utensil washing points
- Ample water points around the site
- Children's adventure playground
- Dogs welcome – exercise area available

Tel: 01395 263170

e-mail: stjohns.farm@virgin.net

www.stjohnsfarm.co.uk

Dawlish, Ilfracombe

symbols

 Holiday Parks & Centres

 Caravans for Hire

 Caravan Sites and Touring Parks

 Camping Sites

Hidden Valley
Touring & camping

This 5 star, family run park is set in a beautiful wooded valley, among rolling hills of stunning Devon countryside. Some of the country's most prestigious beaches are just 4 miles away, including Woolacombe and Putsborough Sands. Overlooking the gardens & stream is the licensed shop and a delightful coffee-shop - perfect after a forest walk!

- Luxury 5* facilities • Children's play parks • Coffee shop • Licensed shop
- Wi-Fi • Tourist information area • Dishwashing areas & launderettes
- Bus stop at entrance to site • Dog exercise field • Woodland walks

Ilfracombe's only **5 star** campsite!

Hidden Valley Park, West Down, Nr. Ilfracombe, North Devon EX34 8NU

01271 813 837 • info@hiddenvalleypark.com

Open all year!

www.hiddenvalleypark.com

Salcombe Regis

Camping & Caravan Park
Sidmouth, Devon EX10 0JH
Tel: 01395 514303
Fax: 01395 514314
contact@salcombe-regis.co.uk
www.salcombe-regis.co.uk

Large Amenities Block
- FREE hot water to all Showers and Basins
- Shaver Points • Dishwashing Area
- Laundrette • Ironing facilities
- Hairdryers • Family Bathroom
- Baby Changing facilities

Shop and Reception
- Information Area • Payphone
- Calor Gas and Camping Gaz sales/refills
- Battery charging service • Basic camping supplies
- Basic General Stores • Freezer Pack Service
- Daily Newspapers (to order only) • Park Post Box

On Site
- Electric Hook-ups
- Chemical and Grey Water Disposal Points
- Children's Playground •Putting Green
- Badminton Net • Large Dog Exercise Field
- Barbeques permitted (NOT disposables)
- Parking on Departure Day (off pitch, small charge)
- Caravan storage subject to availability

The Hook Family Welcomes You

Adjoining our family home and covering 16 acres, Salcombe Regis Camping and Caravan Park offers unrivalled space and tranquillity.

Beautiful views of the combe, with the sea beyond, can be seen from our camping field where young and old may enjoy open expanses of grass ideal for picnics, ball games, flying a kite or just quiet reflection.

Paths lead to the world heritage coast, where Salcombe Mouth boasts a delightful pebble beach, forming part of the Jurassic Coastline, which at low tide gives access to Weston and Sidmouth beaches.

FREE COLOUR BROCHURE

Seaton

Beautiful views, first class facilities, and just a short walk from both the town and the beach, Axevale is the perfect choice for an easy going, relaxing holiday in Devon.

A quiet, family-run park with 68 modern and luxury caravans for hire.
The park overlooks the delightful River Axe Valley, and is just a 10 minute walk from the town with its wonderfully long, award-winning beach.

Ideal for children and families

The park is fenced and safe for children, who will love our extensive play area, with its sand pit, paddling pool, swings and slide.
A reliable babysitting service is available so you can enjoy an evening out on your own

Quiet and peaceful

With no clubhouse, a relaxing atmosphere is ensured.
All of our caravans have a shower, toilet, fridge and TV.
Sited on hard standing which connect dry pathways and tarmac roads. Axevale is the perfect choice in spring and autumn too.

Shopping and Laundry

Laundry facilities are provided and there is a wide selection of goods on sale in the park shop which is open every day.

Prices from £90 per week; reductions for three or fewer persons.

Axevale Caravan Park, Colyford Road, Seaton, Devon EX12 2DF
Tel: 0800 0688816
e-mail: info@axevale.co.uk www.axevale.co.uk

Riverside Caravan & Camping Park
Marsh Lane, North Molton Road,
South Molton, North Devon EX36 3HQ

A beautiful, family-owned caravan and camping park in 40 acres of flat meadow and woodland near the market town of South Molton, an ideal base for exploring Exmoor.

- Luxurious heated shower and toilet block with free hot showers.
- Laundry facilities and baby changing area.
- Children and pets welcome.
- Specimen carp fishing lakes.
- Coarse fishing lakes
- Tearoom with meals.
- Barbecue and picnic tables.
- Hard standing, level Europitches.
- Electrical hook-up.
- Drinking water and grey waste outlet
- TV aerial sockets.
- Large open flat field available for rallies.
- Static caravans for hire.
- Storage available

Tel: 01769 579269
relax@exmoorriverside.co.uk
www.exmoorriverside.co.uk

Woolacombe

Dorset

Bere Regis

CAMPING SITES

DORCHESTER near. Home Farm, Rectory Lane, **Puncknowle, Near Dorchester DT2 9BW (01308 897258).** Small secluded site in beautiful area, one-and-a-half-miles from Heritage Coast, South West Coastal Path, sea fishing; Abbotsbury Swannery nearby; leisure pool, water sports, golf course are within 6 miles. Fossil hunting along the coast; many castles and gardens to visit. We can accommodate tents, touring caravans, motor caravans, trailer tents. Facilities include showers, washbasins, toilets, hairdryers, chemical toilet disposal point, electric hook-ups, gas exchange. Village inn nearby. Open 1st April to end of first week in October. Please pre-book.
- Well behaved dogs welcome, must be on a lead at all times.

FREE or **REDUCED RATE** entry to Holiday Visits and Attractions – see our **READERS' OFFER VOUCHERS** on pages 175-186

Please note...

All the information in this book is given in good faith in the belief that it is correct. However, the publishers cannot guarantee the facts given in these pages, neither are they responsible for changes in policy, ownership or terms that may take place after the date of going to press. Readers should always satisfy themselves that the facilities they require are available and that the terms, if quoted, still apply.

Poole

Set in over 20 acres of tranquil parkland, South Lytchett Manor is the ideal base for exploring the heritage coastline, outstanding local countryside and attractions. It is a friendly, family-run park just three miles from Poole, offering top quality amenities. A local village pub with restaurant just 10 mins walk.

NEW off-lead dog walking for 2012

• Practical Caravan's Best Park in Dorset, 2012 for the fifth year running! • Saver season rates • Shop • Outstanding new heated accessible amenity blocks • New deluxe fully serviced pitches • Free TV connections • Hardstandings • Electric hook-ups • AA pet-friendly dog walk • Regular bus service from main gates • New conservation and information centre • Free Wi-Fi.

Call our booking line on
01202 622577
www.southlytchettmanor.co.uk

South Lytchett Manor
A picture perfect break at any time of year

SOUTH LYTCHETT MANOR

South Lytchett Manor Caravan and Camping Park
Dorchester Road, Lytchett Minster, Poole, Dorset BH16 6JB.
Telephone: 01202 622577. Web: southlytchettmanor.co.uk
Email: info@southlytchettmanor.co.uk

Beacon Hill Touring Park

David Bellamy Gold Award Winners since 2001

Beacon Hill Touring Park enjoys the beauty of 30 acres of partly wooded heathland, together with a wide selection of wildlife. We are a Conservation Award winning park, three miles west of Poole town centre, and just five miles from some of the best beaches Britain has to offer.

- Well stocked shop
- Showers with free hot water
- Baby changing unit
- Laundry rooms with adjacent dishwashing facilities
- Electric hook-ups
- Ample water, waste and chemical disposal points
- Wireless internet
- Heated swimming pool
- Games rooms
- Children's adventure play areas
- All-weather tennis court
- Fishing, with horse riding nearby
- Take-Away/Coffee Shop
- Fully licensed bar

Our natural landscaping affords many unique pitch settings; a non-regimented feel is an aspect our customers return to enjoy.

Beacon Hill Touring Park, Blandford Road North, Poole, Dorset BH16 6AB
Tel: 01202 631631 • Fax: 01202 624388
www.beaconhilltouringpark.co.uk • bookings@beaconhilltouringpark.co.uk

Wareham

West Bexington-on-Sea, Wimborne, Wool

Gloucestershire

Lower Wick, Slimbridge

Somerset

Bridgwater

Martock

SOUTHFORK CARAVAN PARK
• M A R T O C K • S O M E R S E T •

on the edge of the Somerset Levels
Caravans • Motor Homes • Tents • Trailer Tents

Our touring park in beautiful Somerset has level pitches with open views across the countryside but are within easy reach of the facilities on site.
Ideal base for exploring Somerset and within easy reach of the Dorset coastline.
Generous, level pitches for Caravans, Motorhomes and Tents
23 touring pitches (18 with 10amp electric, 5 without electric)
2 serviced pitches (water, 16 amp electric, waste) reinforced geo blocks, grassed over.
2 hard standing gravelled pitches with 16amp electric
Dogs welcome on a short lead
Parking for one car at each pitch
Car park area for extra cars and visitors
Ample space for awning and pods
Pup tents allowed near units

• Our three Atlas Holiday Homes are modern and fully equipped.
• You can book weekends and midweek
• Open all year including Christmas and New Year.
• No smoking or pets.

For further details please contact
Mr & Mrs M.A. Broadley.
Southfork Caravan Park
Parrett Works, Martock
Somerset TA12 6AE
e-mail: info@southforkcaravans.co.uk
www.southforkcaravans.co.uk

Our site facilities include:-
• Heated shower and toilet block - with free showers
• Laundry room with ironing facilities
• Dishwashing sinks separate from clothes washing
• Chemical disposal point
• Play area • Dog exercise area
• Provisions shop - with Local Produce • Off-licence
• Telephone • E-Top ups for mobiles
• Tourist information leaflets

Minehead

PORLOCK CARAVAN PARK

HIGH BANK, PORLOCK, NEAR MINEHEAD, SOMERSET TA24 8ND

- Small, family-run, multi award-winning park
- A few minutes' walk from Porlock village, set in the heart of Exmoor
- Luxury, central heated holiday homes for hire and sale
- Full facilities for tourers, tents and motorhomes
- Village offers several pubs, restaurants and shops selling local produce
- Ideal base from which to explore Exmoor, whether walking, cycling or riding

Facilities on Site include: • Reception & Information Area
- Free Showers and hot water
- Hair dryer and shaver points • Disabled facilities
- Dishwashing room • Laundry room and drying area
- Microwave oven • Free freezer block facility
- Electric hook-up • WiFi
- Grass or hardstanding pitches
- Chemical waste disposal room
- Dog exercise area • Cars park beside units

Phone for brochure 01643 862269
or e-mail: info@porlockcaravanpark.co.uk
www.porlockcaravanpark.co.uk

Porlock

Quantock Orchard Caravan Park

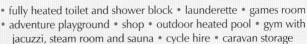

Award-winning, family-run campsite set amidst the stunning Somerset countryside.

Quantock Orchard is situated in an idyllic setting surrounded by picturesque views of the Quantocks, in an Area of Outstanding Natural Beauty. This peaceful park is close to Exmoor, the coast and the West Somerset Railway. Relax and unwind among these beautiful surroundings whilst enjoying our Five Star facilities.

• fully heated toilet and shower block • launderette • games room • adventure playground • shop • outdoor heated pool • gym with jacuzzi, steam room and sauna • cycle hire • caravan storage

Tents, tourers and motorhomes welcome
Luxury static holiday homes for sale or hire
Open all year

Michael & Sara Barrett,
Quantock Orchard Caravan Park, Flaxpool,
Crowcombe, Near Taunton TA4 4AW
01984 618618
e-mail: qocp@flaxpool.freeserve.co.uk
www.quantock-orchard.co.uk

DE LUXE PARK

Ashe Farm

Touring Park

Thornfalcon, Taunton,
Somerset TA3 5NW
TEL: 01823 443764
e-mail: info@ashefarm.co.uk
www.ashefarm.co.uk

Ashe Farm Touring Park is a quiet, informal family-run site, part of a working farm situated in the Vale of Taunton between the Quantock and Blackdown Hills. The six acre site has two sheltered meadows with lovely views of the hills and an atmosphere of peace and seclusion. Towing approach from the M5 motorway is easy and the site is easy to find at the end of your journey.

There are electric hook-ups in both fields. The first field has a new toilet block with showers, hot water, hair dryers and razor points. There are toilet facilities for the disabled and a laundry with tumble dryer and iron. Nearby is the Information Room and a play area for small children, also wash up sinks and waste disposal points.

TOURING & CAMPING PARK

Wiltshire

London
(Central & Greater)

London has it all - theatres, shopping, concerts, museums, art galleries, pageantry and sporting events. There's plenty to see and do, from all the hands on activities of the Science Museum and the Natural History Museum, the National Gallery with one of the largest art collections in the world, the thought-provoking artworks at the Tate Modern, the splendour of Buckingham Palace and the magnificent gardens at Kew, to a sumptuous afternoon tea at a top hotel. With a wide range of accommodation at prices to suit every pocket, it's easy to spend a weekend here or a take a longer break.

Maidenhead

Berkshire

HURLEY RIVERSIDE PARK

Family-run Park situated in the picturesque village of Hurley alongside the River Thames. Ideally located for visiting LEGOLAND Windsor®, Oxford, Henley-on-Thames and London

Gold David Bellamy Conservation Award winning park
Tourers, motorhomes, RVs and tents welcome
Grass, hard-standing and premium multi-service pitches
Free shower blocks including family shower rooms
Launderette • Shop • Disabled facilities
Nature trail • Slipway • Riverside picnic grounds
Fishing in season • Fully-serviced Caravan
Holiday Homes and ReadyTents for hire
• Discounted LEGOLAND® tickets available
• Open 1st March–31st October

 Find us on Facebook

HURLEY, BERKSHIRE SL6 5NE
TEL: 01628 824493

www.hurleyriversidepark.co.uk • info@hurleyriversidepark.co.uk

Just a short train ride away from central London, in Berkshire explore historic towns and villages, wander by the tranquil waters of the River Thames, visit gardens and great houses, like Basildon Park at Pangbourne. Windsor Castle is always major attraction, or have a fun day out at the races at nearby Ascot. Children will love Legoland, and the hands-on science at the Look Out Discovery Centre at Bracknell.

FREE or REDUCED RATE entry to Holiday Visits and Attractions –
see our **READERS' OFFER VOUCHERS** on pages 175-186

Wellington Country Park Campsite, located between Reading and Basingstoke on the A33, offers you the opportunity to pitch within the beauty and tranquillity of woodland, with open parkland, lakes and nature trails to explore.

Easily reached from both the M3 and M4 motorways, it is ideal both as a touring base and a destination.

The shower block provides free showers, toilets, shaver points, hairdryers and laundry.

Included within your fee is FREE unlimited access to all the Country Park facilities, with

adventure play areas, miniature railways, sand pits, slides, crazy golf, a nature trail maze, and animal farm and petting barn (seasonal).

Definitely a campsite for all the family!

Wokingham

Beaconsfield

Buckinghamshire

Quiet, level meadowland park. Ideal for touring London, train station one mile. 25 minutes to Marylebone, cheap day return fares available. Legoland 12 miles, with Windsor Castle and the Thames. Model village three miles, many local attractions, including rare breeds farm. Local inn for food quarter of a mile. Lots of walks, ideal for dogs. En suite accommodation available – room only. New shower block and tenting area. 65 pitches available. Open March to January.

Tourers from £17 to £36, tents from £15, motor homes £17 to £36, electric point £3.50

HIGHCLERE FARM
New Barn Lane, Seer Green, Near Beaconsfield, Bucks HP9 2QZ

Tel & Fax: 01494 874505
e-mail: highclerepark@aol.com
www.highclerefarmpark.co.uk

While every effort is made to ensure accuracy, we regret that FHG Guides cannot accept responsibility for errors, misrepresentations or omissions in our entries or any consequences thereof. Prices in particular should be checked. We will follow up complaints but cannot act as arbiters or agents for either party.

Fordingbridge

Hampshire

HILL COTTAGE FARM CAMPING & CARAVAN PARK

*Regional winners for South East England 2012
Practical Caravan Top 100 Sites.*

Set in 40 acres of glorious countryside close to the New Forest, this lovely privately owned site offers fully serviced, generous sized hardstanding pitches with dividing hedges Amenity barn with toilets, free showers including disabled; laundry room and information room. Free Wi-Fi on certain pitches and in information room. A well kept camping field with toilet facilities, dishwashing, electric hook ups and play area. Woodland walks from site leading to local village pub and store • Bournemouth beaches 30 min drive.

Open 1st March - 30th November. Rallies welcome all year.

**Sandleheath Road, Alderholt, Fordingbridge, Hants SP6 3EG
Telephone: 01425 650513 • Fax: 01425 652339
info@hillcottagefarmcampingandcaravanpark.co.uk
www.hillcottagefarmcampingandcaravanpark.co.uk**

Idyllic countryside, sandy beaches, beautiful gardens and historic houses, country parks, museums and castles, and wildlife parks, are all there to enjoy in Hampshire. There are museums full of military heritage on land, sea and air, including the HMS Victory at Portsmouth, where a trip to the top of the Spinnaker Tower provides spectacular views of the surrounding area. Outdoors walk, cycle or ride on horseback over the heathland and through the ancient woodlands of the New Forest, and in the South Downs National Park, or try out one of the many watersports available along the coast. Boating enthusiasts will make for one of the many marinas, and the annual regatta on the River Hamble, and for courses on sailing, rockclimbing, and even skiing, where better to learn more than the Calshot Activities Centre on the shores of the Solent.

WELCOME TO HAYLING ISLAND
FAMILY CAMP SITES

Hayling Island is an ideal touring base for Portsmouth, the Isle of Wight and the New Forest, with excellent motorway access.

We are a small family-run company with two well established sites on the Island. The Oven is the larger of the two with approximately 350 pitches.

We offer good value for money and cater for caravans, tents and motorhomes, all on grass pitches.

Our facilities include a Children's play area, Shop and Café on site, games room, heated swimming pool (extra charge applies), Level sheltered marked pitches, toilets and showers included, boat washing facility. Pool open from Easter to September. Private pool hire available.

Ideally situated near the sea, with excellent water sports available close by. The site is easy to find and signposted from the main road.

We are also able to cater for rallies at The Oven, please phone to enquire about dates and prices.

Standard sites £17.50 (including VAT) per night for car/tent or caravan and two people.
To book please send £22.50 (£20 deposit and £2.50 booking fee) also SAE if confirmation required.

The Oven Campsite
Manor Road, Hayling Island PO11 0QX
Tel: 023 9246 4695
Mobile: 077584 10020
Out of Hours: 02392 465850
(leave message if no reply).
e-mail: theovencampsite@talktalk.net
www.haylingcampsites.co.uk

Romsey, Southsea

Biddenden

Kent

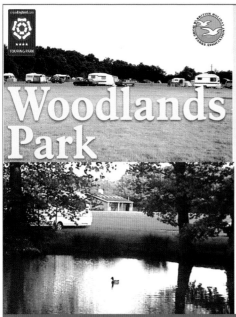

Situated in the heart of the beautiful Kent countryside, a quiet and tranquil environment to enjoy your holiday.
An ideal base for visiting the many historic Castles and other attractions throughout Kent and East Sussex.
Large open level grassland park with two ponds to enjoy a spot of fishing
Electric hook-ups available, modern toilet and shower block facility.
Plenty of space for children to run around and let off steam.
Small site shop where all essential items can be purchased from camping gaz to a bottle of milk. Friendly staff are on hand to answer any questions on the area and to provide tourist information.

**Tenterden Road,
Biddenden, Kent TN27 8BT
Tel: 01580 291216
e-mail: woodlandspark@
             overlinebroadband.com
www.campingsite.co.uk**

Residential Park Homes, Leisure Homes and Tourist Park

symbols

	Holiday Parks & Centres
	Caravans for Hire
	Caravan Sites and Touring Parks
	Camping Sites

Birchington

Two Chimneys
Caravan Park

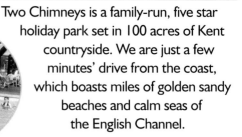

Two Chimneys is a family-run, five star holiday park set in 100 acres of Kent countryside. We are just a few minutes' drive from the coast, which boasts miles of golden sandy beaches and calm seas of the English Channel.

In recent years Two Chimneys Caravan Park has undergone a large amount of expansion and improvement providing more modern facilities, Toilets, Showers, Launderette and a Telescopic Swimming Pool Enclosure, so the pool can still be enjoyed on those not so warm days.

Licensed Club House, on-site Shop, The Grove Diner, Tennis Court, Children's Play Areas. Holiday hire also available.

Two Chimneys has over 200 tent and touring pitches available on level grass fields. Open from March to October. Sorry no dogs.

Telephone:
01843 841068 / 843157
Fax: 01843 848099
Two Chimneys Caravan Park
Shottendane Road,
Birchington,
Kent CT7 0HD

www.twochimneys.co.uk

Battle, Bodiam

East Sussex

Fairfields Farm

Caravan & Camping Park

Eastbourne Road, Westham, Pevensey BN24 5NG
Tel: 01323 763165
e-mail: enquiries@fairfieldsfarm.com
www.fairfieldsfarm.com

Quiet country touring site on a working family-run farm.
Close to the beautiful resort of Eastbourne, we offer an excellent base from which to explore the stunning scenery and diverse attractions of South East England. Our farm spans an area of over 200 acres, and alongside the extensive views you will find a duck pond, numerous farm animals and pets, a recreational walk and a fishing lake.

Site open from 1st April to 31st October.

Special Low Season Midweek Offer
3 nights for the price of 2
Please contact us for further details

From the dramatic cliffs and sandy beaches of the Sussex coast to the quiet countryside
of the Weald and the South Downs, there's an endless choice of the things to do and
places to explore. Sailing, walking, cycling, horse riding, golf are all available for an active
break, while the fascinating history of 1066 country, castles like Bodiam and the seaside
ports will attract all the family. If you're looking for beaches, the 100 miles of coast offer
something for everyone, whether your preference is for action-packed fun at a family
resort or a quiet, remote spot. Best known for a combination of lively nightlife and all the
attractions of the seaside, Brighton has everything from its pebble beach, classic pier,
Royal Pavilion and Regency architecture, to shopping malls, art galleries, antique shops,
and the specialist boutiques and coffee shops of The Lanes. There's so much to choose from!

Chichester

West Sussex

Honeybridge Park

A picturesque 15-acre touring, camping and caravan park set in an Area of Outstanding Natural Beauty, convenient for London, Gatwick & South Coast.

Large hardstanding and grass pitches, electric hook-ups, heated amenity blocks, licensed shop, laundry, games room and play area. Seasonal pitches. Tourer storage. Caravan for hire. Luxury lodges and static caravans for sale on 11-month holiday licences. Dogs welcome. Open all year.

Tel: 01403 710923
web: www.honeybridgepark.co.uk
e-mail: enquiries@honeybridgepark.co.uk
Honeybridge Lane, Dial Post, Horsham, West Sussex RH13 8NX

enjoyEngland.com ★★★★ HOLIDAY PARK

AA ►►►► 🚐🚐⛺

Essex

From the historic port of Harwich in the north to the Thames estuary in the south, the 300 miles of coastline and dry climate of maritime Essex have attracted holiday makers since early Victorian times. Nowadays there's plenty for everyone - fun family resorts with plenty of action like Clacton, on the Essex sunshine coast, and Southend-on-Sea, with over six miles of clean safe sand and the world's longest pleasure pier. At Maldon take a trip on a Thames barge to see the seal colonies or cross the Saxon causeway to Mersea Island to taste the oysters, washed down by wine produced on the vineyard there, but watch the tides! Yachting is a favourite pastime at Burnham-on-Crouch, but for land-based transport visit the railway museum with working locomotives. Keen gardeners can visit the restored and preserved gardens at Audley End, Easton Lodge and Hylands House or the contemporary designs of Beth Chatto's gravel, water and woodland gardens near Colchester.

Norfolk

Along the Norfolk coast from King's Lynn to Great Yarmouth the broad, sandy beaches, grassy dunes, nature reserves, windmills, and pretty little fishing villages are inviting at all times of year. Following the routes of the Norfolk Coastal Path and Norfolk Coast Cycle Way, walk or cycle between the picturesque villages, stopping to visit the interesting shops and galleries, or to enjoy the seafood at a traditional pub or a restaurant. Take lessons in surfing at Wells-next-the-Sea, then enjoy the challenge of the waves at East Runton or Cromer, or go sea fishing here, or at Sheringham or Mundesley. An important trade and fishing port from medieval times, the historic centre of King's Lynn is well worth a visit, and take a break at Great Yarmouth for family entertainment, 15 miles of sandy beaches, traditional piers, a sea life centre and nightlife with clubs and a casino.

WAVENEY VALLEY HOLIDAY PARK

★ Touring Caravan and Camping Site ★ Licensed Bar ★ Electric Hook-ups
★ Restaurant, Shop, Laundry ★ Self-Catering Mobile Homes
★ Outdoor Swimming Pool ★ Horse Riding on Site ★ Good Fishing in Locality

Good access to large, level site, two miles east of Dickleburgh.
Midway between Norwich and Ipswich off A140.

Airstation Lane, Rushall, Diss,
Norfolk IP21 4QF
Telephone: 01379 741228/741690
Fax: 01379 741228
e-mail: waveneyvalleyhp@aol.com
www.caravanparksnorfolk.co.uk

Willowcroft
Camping and Caravan Park

A small, very friendly, family run 2-acre site set in peaceful unspoilt surroundings.
Just a two-minute walk from the river, where you can fish, sail, row, or simply walk
along the river bank into Potter Heigham Village, only twenty minutes away.

We are only 15 miles from both
Norwich and Great Yarmouth, with a
selection of wonderful beaches only 5
or so miles away. The site itself offers
showers, toilets, electric hook-ups,
welcomes dogs and is an ideal haven
for bird watchers, cyclists
and walkers.

Willowcroft Camping And Caravan Park
Staithe Road, Repps-with-Bastwick, Great Yarmouth NR29 5JU • Tel: 01692 670380
e-mail: willowcroftsite@btinternet.com • www.willowcroft.net

Sandy Gulls Caravan Park

Found on the Mundesley cliff tops, this quiet private park, managed by the owning family for over 30 years, offers a warm welcome to all visitors.

The touring park has 35 grass and non-turf pitches, all have uninterrupted sea views, electric/TV hook-ups and beautifully refurbished shower rooms.

Holiday caravans for sale or hire, which are always the latest models. Superbly situated for exploring the beauty of North Norfolk including The Broads National Park.
Open March to November. Wi-Fi.
Touring caravan park is adults only.

Cromer Road, Mundesley
Norfolk NR11 8DF

Samantha **01263 720513**

info@sandygulls.co.uk
www.sandygulls.co.uk

Weybourne

Bolding Way Holidays

We're in the pretty coastal village of Weybourne, close to the towns of Sheringham & Holt. We are just a 12-minute walk to the sea. The campsite is private and secluded, within easy reach of the coast - perfect for walkers, cyclists, bird watchers, fisherman & dog walkers. There is an excellent village shop, café & pub within 200 yards. Tents, trailer tent & small campervans are welcome. We also have two Mongolian Yurts, with everything you need for a self-catering holiday. They each have their own private garden, brazier & bbq. The campsite has shared use of our hot tub & sauna. There are just 12 pitches, some with elec. Open from Easter to Oct 1/2 term. There are toilets, showers & kitchen area. We also have holiday cottages available.

clothes are optional!

Bolding Way Holidays. The Barn, Bolding Way, Weybourne, Holt, Norfolk
Phone: 01263 588 666   website: www.BoldingWay.co.uk.

Suffolk

Lowestoft

Pakefield
:::caravan park

The perfect location to enjoy aspectacular stretch of the SunriseCoast, this clifftop park enjoyswonderful views, fresh salty airand direct access to a beautifulshingle beach. The sound of seaon shingle has a soothing resonance which adds to the pleasure of a holiday at Pakefield.

PAKEFIELD CARAVAN PARK
Arbor Lane, Lwestoft, Suffolk NR33 7BE
01502 561136
pakefieldpark.cco.uk

FOUR STAR
HOLIDAY & CARAVAN
PARKS
★★★★
coastdaleparks

Outney Meadow Caravan Park

This caravan and camping site in Suffolk is in a beautiful location, set in eight acres of ground on pleasant grassy areas beside the River Waveney, with screened pitches for tents, motor homes and caravans.

Toilets and shower block with hot showers and shaver points. Shop and launderette on site.

45 touring pitches and five hardstandings for motor caravans; some electric hook-ups.

Fishing, boat, canoe and bike hire. Barbecues are allowed; picnic tables. Pets welcome, special dog-walking area; dogs must be kept on leads.

The site is quiet day and night.

Please telephone or see our website for further details.

**Outney Meadow,
Bungay, Suffolk NR35 1HG
Tel: 01986 892338
www.outneymeadow.co.uk**

Cakes & Ale — HOLIDAY PARK

The ideal base from which to explore the stunning **Suffolk coast** and countryside, or just relax and put your feet up.

01728 831655   www.cakesandale.co.uk   reception@cakesandale.co.uk

Buxton

Derbyshire

For walking, climbing, cycling, horse riding, mountain biking and caving, visit Derbyshire. Take part in one of the walking festivals, with themed walks at every level, cycle the recently restored Monsal Trail through spectacular scenery along the old railway line from Bakewell to Buxton, or hire an electric bike to enjoy the countryside, whatever your level of fitness. Visit Poole's Cavern to see the best stalagmites and stalactites in Derbyshire (and discover the difference!), and the Blue John Cave at Castleton where this rare mineral is mined, and perhaps buy a sample of jewellery in one of the local shops. Buxton was a spa from Roman times, but the main attractions now are concerts, theatre and the opera, music and literature festival held every year. Go to Wirksworth in spring for the annual well dressings or try out a wizard's wand at Hardwick Hall near Chesterfield, the market town with the church with the crooked spire.

Please note...

All the information in this book is given in good faith in the belief that it is correct.
However, the publishers cannot guarantee the facts given in these pages, neither
are they responsible for changes in policy, ownership or terms that may take place
after the date of going to press. Readers should always satisfy themselves that the
facilities they require are available and that the terms, if quoted, still apply.

The FHG Directory of Website Addresses
on pages 167-173 is a useful quick reference guide for
holiday accommodation with e-mail and/or website details

FREE or **REDUCED RATE** entry to Holiday Visits and Attractions –
see our **READERS' OFFER VOUCHERS** on pages 175 -186

Ripley

Golden Valley
Caravan & Camping Park

Coach Road, Golden Valley, Ripley, Derbyshire DE55 4ES
Tel: 01773 513881 • Fax: 01773 746786
e-mail: enquiries@goldenvalleycaravanpark.co.uk
www.goldenvalleycaravanpark.co.uk

Golden Valley Caravan and Camping Park is located in the beautiful hamlet of Golden Valley, in Amber Valley, the heart of Derbyshire. Next to Butterley Railway. Set within 26 acres of secluded woodland and contains 40 super pitches for motor homes/caravans each having its own independent water supply, electric hook-up point and mains drainage set in spacious bays within selected areas. There is also ample room for camping/tents with hook-ups.

The site has two independent toilet / shower blocks, laundry room, Jacuzzi, gym, children's play room, outside play area, cafe, bar and fishing pond.

Amber Valley has many tranquil villages and bustling market towns nestled amongst some of the most beautiful scenery around. From historic houses and heritage sites, steam trains to walking routes there's something for you.

Wolvey

Leicestershire & Rutland

Wolvey Caravan Park
Villa Farm

Caravan & Camping Site

**Villa Farm, Wolvey,
Near Hinckley
Leicestershire LE10 3HF**

A quiet site situated on the borders of Warwickshire and Leicestershire, ideally located to explore the many places of interest in the Midlands. Site facilities include shop (licensed), toilets, disabled unit, showers, washrooms, launderette, TV room, 9 hole putting green, fishing.

Tariff and brochure available on request. Registered with the Caravan and Camping Club of Great Britain.

Tel: 01455 220493/220630

www.wolveycaravanpark.itgo.com

Set in the centre of the Midlands, the rolling countryside, canals, forests, beautiful villages, interesting market towns and history make Leicestershire and Rutland well worth a visit. In the north west the 200 square miles of the new National Forest, joining the ancient woodlands of Needham and Charnwood, are transforming the landscape and giving access to this wide stretch of countryside to walkers, cyclists and horse riders. With over 1000 different species there's plenty to see at Twycross Zoo at Hinckley, or take a walk through Burbage Wood to see the native fauna. Snibston Country Park and Grange Nature Reserve have been established on the site of a former colliery, and as well as outdoor activities there's an interactive science museum where everyone can learn and have fun at the same time. Rutland is England's smallest county with the largest man-made lake in Europe. Cycle round the shoreline, cruise on the water, watch the bird life or walk round the lake, while the really energetic can take the walkers' route, The Rutland Round.

Boston

Lincolnshire

Alford

Boston, Market Rasen

Tuxford

Nottinghamshire

Orchard Park Touring Caravan and Camping Park
Marnham Road, Tuxford NG22 OPY
Tel: 01777 870228 • Fax: 01777 870320

Orchard Park

Quiet, sheltered Park set in an old orchard. Ideal for Sherwood Forest and many attractions, all pitches with electric hook-up, children's play trail, dog walk, excellent heated facilities with free hot showers and facilities for disabled. Brochure available on request.

www.orchardcaravanpark.co.uk

In Nottinghamshire the myths, legends and facts all play a part in the stories of Robin Hood, but visit Sherwood Forest, the hiding place of outlaws in medieval times, and make up your own mind from the evidence you find there. Watch cricket at Trent Bridge, horse racing at Nottingham and the all-weather course at Southwell, and ice hockey at Nottingham's National Ice Centre, or try ice skating yourself. There are golf courses from municipal and pay & play to championship standard, fishing in canals, lakes and fisheries, walking by rivers and canals and cycling in the woodland and country parks, and everyone is welcome to play at the Nottingham Tennis Centre. The city of Nottingham is a wonderful place to shop, with designer outlets, independent shops and department stores, and don't miss the traditional Lace Market.

symbols

☼	*Holiday Parks & Centres*
	Caravans for Hire
	Caravan Sites and Touring Parks
	Camping Sites

Greenacres caravan park

Greenacres is a family-owned and run holiday park in North Nottinghamshire, often referred to as a 'gem set in the heart of Robin Hood Country'. Facilities available for tourers, motorhomes, small tents etc.
Static holiday homes for sale and hire.
Seasonal touring caravan pitches available.
Open mid March to end of October.

Lincoln Road, Tuxford
Nottinghamshire NG22 0JN
Tel & Fax: 01777 870264
e: stay@greenacres-tuxford.co.uk
www.greenacres-tuxford.co.uk

Leominster

Herefordshire

Riverside Caravan Site
at Eaton Court Farm

A level site set in a countryside location, on the outskirts of Leominster.
Facilities include: drinking water, electric hook-ups, waste disposal point, electric shower, flush toilet, handwash basin with oversink heater. Tents welcome. Two golf courses nearby, fishing on the Lugg and scenic walks. Castles, historic houses and gardens, the Mappa Mundi at Hereford and Hay-on-Wye bookshops all easily accessible.

**Eaton Court Farm, Stoke Prior Road,
Leominster, Herefordshire HR6 0NA
Tel: 01568 612095**

Outdoor activities, creative arts and crafts, wonderful food - Herefordshire, on the border with Wales, will appeal whatever your interest. With its rolling countryside and green meadows dotted with woodland and meandering streams, there are endless opportunities for all kinds of outdoor activities, from white water canoeing on the Yat Rapids through the steep-sided gorge at Symonds Yat, to longer, more gentle trips on the quieter sections of the River Wye. Footpaths, bridleways and traffic-free cycle trails through countryside rich in wildlife are perfect for families as well as the more experienced. The Black and White Village Trail takes visitors through beautiful countryside to pretty little villages, each with its own individual characteristics and shops, or follow the Cider Route in this county of apple orchards.

Marston

West Midlands

Warwickshire

The West Midlands, with Birmingham its hub, is the focus of all transport networks in central England so that access is easy by road, rail and air. Once there, cycle or walk alongside the network of canals, tracing the development of industrialisation in the Black Country west of Birmingham and visiting the museums which give visitors an insight into the different industries which grew up in the area, based on the abundant coal supplies. In Birmingham's vibrant centre there's plenty to do. Shopping has to be high on the agenda, with a wide variety of choice from malls to markets, high quality department stores, and the well established specialist jewellery quarter. There are art galleries and concerts, and art, dance and music festivals to go to, as well as major international events and exhibitions to appeal to everyone, from gardeners to jazz lovers, and the major athletics and tennis events, not forgetting football and cricket of course. Unravel the mysteries of space at the Thinktank Planetarium or experience the thrills of go-karting – something for every age group.

We are a small, family run park, very clean and fairly quiet. Set in lovely countryside, just two miles south west of Stratford-upon-Avon. An ideal location to visit the numerous Cotswold villages with their thatched inns, Shakespeare's birthplace and Warwick Castle. There are country walks to the River Avon and the village of Luddington. On leaving Stratford-upon-Avon take B439 signposted Bidford for two miles. You will find us on the left after going over a large hill.

Over 50 years as a family business.

A warm welcome awaits!

Dodwell Park is very well equipped to make your camping stay homely and comfortable. These are some of our facilities: -
Toilets • Free hot showers • Washhand basins with hot water
Hand and hair dryers • Shaving points
Calor and Camping Gaz • Dishwashing facilities
Shop and off-licence • Hard standings • Electric hook-ups
Public telephone and post box • Dogs are welcome

**Evesham Road (B439)
Stratford-upon-Avon
Warwickshire
CV37 9SR**

**Tel: 01789 204957
enquiries@dodwellpark.co.uk
www.dodwellpark.co.uk**

North Yorkshire

Gristhorpe, Near Filey YO14 9PS

Situated on the glorious Yorkshire coast between Scarborough and Filey. Privately owned and operated, this Rose award-winning park is a perfect base for families and couples wishing to make the most of these two great seaside towns and their glorious sandy beaches.

- Heated Indoor Swimming Pool
- Lounge Bar / Family Bar
- Supermarket
- Games Room
- Fish & Chip Takeaway
- Children's Play Area
- Pot Wash & Laundry
- Wi-Fi

Touring Caravans, Motorhomes and Tents welcome.

e-mail: enquiries@crowsnestcaravanpark.com
Tel: 01723 582206 • www.crowsnestcaravanpark.com

CAMPING SITES

HAWES. Mr and Mrs Facer, Bainbridge Ings Caravan and Camping Site, Hawes DL8 3NU (01969 667354). A quiet, clean, family-run site with beautiful views and only half-a-mile from Hawes. Good centre for walking and touring the Dales. You can be assured of a warm welcome.
Rates: from £14.00 per day.
• Pets welcome. • Children welcome.
ETC ★★★
e-mail: janet@bainbridge-ings.co.uk   www.bainbridge-ings.co.uk

---

FREE or **REDUCED RATE** entry to Holiday Visits and Attractions –
see our **READERS' OFFER VOUCHERS** on pages 175 -186

Harrogate

Hutton Le Hole Caravan Park

A family-run site at Westfield Lodge Farm, on the
southern edge of the North Yorkshire Moors.
A level, free-draining and secluded site with modern facilities
in a picturesque and peaceful location just outside the village of
Hutton Le Hole. This site has on-farm walks and is ideal for
walking the North York Moors and touring the area.
York is one hour's drive and Scarborough and the coast
45 minutes. Castle Howard is 20 minutes' drive away.
Open Easter to 31st October. Prices from £12.50 per night

**Enquiries/brochure: Mrs Annabel Strickland,
Westfield Lodge, Hutton Le Hole YO62 6UG
Tel: 01751 417261 • Fax: 01751 417876
e-mail: rwstrickland@farmersweekly.net
www.westfieldlodge.co.uk**

Kirkbymoorside, Masham

Otterington Park

Situated in the Vale of York on a family-run farm, Otterington Park is a quality, purpose built 5-acre site designed to cater for up to 40 touring units. Electricity and luxury heated amenity block complete with individual bath/shower rooms, disabled facilities and laundry facilities available. Coarse fishing on site.

Children and dogs welcome!

There is also a brand new development, adjoining the Touring Caravan site, ready for 40 Luxury Holiday Lodges and Static Caravans. Full details on request.

This is an ideal base for visiting the moors and dales of Yorkshire including locations from TV favourites such as *Heartbeat, Brideshead Revisited* and *Emmerdale*, market towns, leisure centres, golf courses, theme parks and other tourist attractions.

**Otterington Park,
Station Farm,
South Otterington, Northallerton DL7 9JB
Tel: 01609 780656
www.otteringtonpark.com • info@otteringtonpark.com**

Pickering, Scarborough

Scarborough

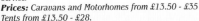

Dominated by the magnificent York Minster, the largest medieval Gothic cathedral in northern Europe, the city of York in North Yorkshire is full of attractions for the visitor. Have fun finding your way through the Snickelways, the maze of hidden alleyways, and enjoy a morning – or longer – in the array of independent shops and boutiques as well as all the top high street stores. Explore York's past at Jorvik, the recreation of the original Viking city from 1000 years ago or become an archaeologist for the day at Dig! and excavate for yourself items from Viking, Roman, medieval and Victorian times.

ADULTS ONLY

Whitby

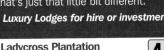

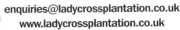

York

Outside the city the vast open stretches of the North York Moors and Yorkshire Dales National Parks and the golden sandy beaches of the coast are perfect for an active holiday. Every standard of fitness and ability is catered for, whether surfing at Scarborough or cycling through Dalby Forest, gliding over the North York Moors National Park or floating in a hot air balloon admiring the scenery at dawn. Gentle, short, circular routes for walkers are centred on interesting, historic stone villages and busy market towns, or cross the countryside on the more demanding long distance trails, like the Cleveland Way, the Pennine Trail and the Dales Way, or the really challenging Yorkshire Three Peaks in Ribblesdale.

FHG Guides publish a large range of well-known accommodation guides. We will be happy to send you details or you can use the order form at the back of this book.

Bamburgh, Hexham

Northumberland

Make the discovery
Holgates

Silverdale Caravan Park

Hard standing fully serviced 5 star pitches open all year

AA Campsite of the Year 2011

Hollins Farm

Beautiful secluded Farm site with hard standing fully serviced pitches

Bay View

Now fully serviced pitches with new extended year round season

To find out more contact us on 01524 701508 or
Email: relax@holgates.co.uk   www.holgates.co.uk

Knutsford

Cheshire

In Cheshire, just south of Manchester, combine a city break in historic Chester with a day or two at one of relaxing spas either in the city itself or in one of the luxury resorts in the rolling countryside. A round at an on-site golf course offers an alternative way of enjoying the break, and while out in the country, why not visit one of the many gardens open to the public? Time your visit to the historic Georgian mansion at Tatton Park to coincide with one of the wide choice of events held there throughout the year, including the annual RHS Flower Show. All the family will be fascinated by a visit to the giant Lovell Telescope at Jodrell Bank Visitor Centre near the old silk weaving town of Macclesfield or a ride on the Anderton Boat Lift at Northwich. The walkways in nearby Delamere Forest provide pleasant and not too challenging walks, or hire a mountain bike to ride round the forest trails.

Warrington

Hollybank Caravan Park

Quiet park in picturesque rural setting.
110 touring pitches, electric hook-ups, modern toilet blocks,
showers and hot water (free), central heating, shop, phone and launderette,
Calor and Gaz, games room.

Ideal base for touring North West, Peak District,
Yorkshire Dales and a convenient night halt off M6, M56, M60.

Open all year. Brochure available.

Directions: two miles east off Junction 21 M6 on A57 (Irlam).
Turn right at lights into Warburton Bridge Road; entry on left.

**Hollybank Caravan Park, Warburton Bridge Road,
Rixton, Warrington WA3 6HU • 0161-775 2842**

Cumbria

Children of all ages will want to visit The Beatrix Potter Attraction at Bowness-on-Windermere and Hilltop, the author's home on the other side of the lake. Find out all about the area at Brockhole, the National Park Visitor Centre overlooking Windermere, with an adventure playground and lovely gardens. For the central Lakes stay at Ambleside or one of the many traditional Lakeland villages, like Grasmere, the home of Wordsworth. The busy market town of Keswick is the ideal centre for exploring the north Lakes, including the historic port of Whitehaven, the former centre for the rum trade. Go back in time with a visit to the Rum Story to understand more about the connection between this and the history of slavery. Stay in Penrith, Appleby-in-Westmorland or Kirkby Lonsdale to explore the western Pennines or Silloth-on-Solway to discover the Solway Firth coast.

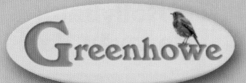

Coniston, Grange-over-Sands, Kendal

Kendal, Keswick

Newby Bri...

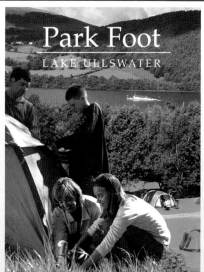

kses
aravan Park

Conveniently situated within six miles of the M6 motorway, this caravan park offers a choice of holiday accommodation on the fringe of the Lake District National Park. Four and six-berth caravans for hire, with mains services, electric light and fridge, gas cooker and fire, toilet, separate double and bunk bedrooms, kitchen area and lounge. Fully equipped except linen. Alternatively those with touring caravans and tents will find excellent facilities on site; toilets, showers, chemical disposal points, stand pipes and laundry facilities. Within easy reach of outdoor heated swimming pool, pony trekking, fishing and fell walking. Some local pubs have restaurant facilities. Full details and terms on request.

AA
▶▶▶
Penruddock, Penrith, Cumbria CA11 0RX
Tel: 017684 83224

Waterside House Campsite

Waterside House, Howtown Road, Pooley Bridge,
Penrith, Cumbria CA10 2NA • Tel & Fax: 017684 86332

Farm and campsite situated about one mile from Pooley Bridge. Genuine Lakeside location with beautiful views of Lake Ullswater and Fells. Ideal for windsurfing, canoeing, boating, fell walking and fishing, table tennis, volleyball. Boat, canoe and mountain bike hire on site. Play area, shop and gas exchange also. SAE or telephone for brochure. Open March to October. Directions: M6 Junction 40, A66 follow signs for Ullswater, A592 to Pooley Bridge, one mile along Howtown Road on right - signposted.

e-mail: enquire@watersidefarm-campsite.co.uk
www.watersidefarm-campsite.co.uk

symbols

☼ *Holiday Parks & Centres*

  Caravans for Hire

  Caravan Sites and Touring Parks

  Camping Sites

Solway Holiday Village

Located in the unspoiled seaside Victorian town of Silloth-on-Solway, this 120-acre family park has something for everyone. A truly idyllic location, the park enjoys breathtaking views out over the Solway Firth to Scotland and offers an ideal touring centre for the Scottish Borders and the English Lake District

Sale & Hiring from £19pppn

Touring Site from £5.95

BOOK NOW on
016973 31236

- Caravans/Lodges with hot tubs
- Indoor Leisure Pool
- Fitness Suite
- Sauna and Jacuzzi
- Tennis Courts
- 9-hole Golf Course
- Licensed Bars
- Live Entertainment
- Kids' Club
- Indoor Play Area
- Outdoor Play Area
- Ten-Pin Bowling
- Pool & Games Room
- Animal Farm
- NEW Italian-themed Courtyard Water Garden
- Tourer from £5.95
- Holiday Homes from £6,995

Solway Holiday Village, Skinburness Drive, Silloth-on-Solway, Wigton, Cumbria CA7 4QQ

solwayenquiries@hagansleisure.co.uk
www.hagansleisure.co.uk

Tanglewood Caravan Park
CAUSEWAY HEAD, SILLOTH-ON-SOLWAY, CUMBRIA CA7 4PE

TANGLEWOOD is a family-run park on the fringes of the Lake District National Park. It is tree-sheltered and situated one mile inland from the small port of Silloth on the Solway Firth, with a beautiful view of the Galloway Hills. Large modern holiday homes are available from March to January, with car parking beside each home. Fully equipped except for bed linen, with central heating, electric lighting, hot and cold water, toilet, shower, gas fire, fridge and colour TV, all of which are included in the tariff. Touring pitches also available with electric hook-ups and water/drainage facilities, etc. Play area. Licensed lounge with adjoining children's play room. Pets welcome free but must be kept under control at all times. Full colour brochure available.

TEL: 016973 31253 • e-mail: tanglewoodcaravanpark@hotmail.com • www.tanglewoodcaravanpark.co.uk

• DOWNLOADABLE BROCHURE WITH TARIFF AND BOOKING FORM AVAILABLE ON WEBSITE. •

Ullswater
Caravan Camping & Marine Park

This quiet and secluded park provides all amenities and home comforts the discerning holiday maker would expect.
Games room • Bar • Washing and ironing facilities
Breathtaking scenery at any time of the year. Some of the best walking country in Britain.
Private marina with access to stunning Lake Ullswater one mile away.
Delightful towns and villages dotted throughout the Lake District and Cumbria.

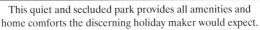

- Electric hook ups available. Camping only areas.
- Static caravans & holiday cottages available to let.
- Cottages are available all year round.
- Static caravans available April-November.

Ullswater Caravan, Camping & Marine Park
Watermillock, Ullswater CA11 0LR
Tel: 017684 86666
e-mail: info@uccmp.co.uk
www.ullswatercaravanpark.co.uk

A truly wonderful location, this single sited modern, static caravan enjoys unspoilt views of the beautiful Whicham Valley. Situated on a working beef/sheep farm at the foot of Backcombe mountain, with plenty of fell and beach walking on our doorstep. The caravan sleeps 4 people in two separate bedrooms, bedding provided. Gas cooking, electric heating and lighting, fridge, microwave and spin dryer. Shower room with basin, w.c. and shaver point. Sorry, no dogs. Ample parking. Terms from £200 to £350 per week. Short breaks out of season

Whicham Hall Farm

Mrs Capstick, Whicham Hall Farm, Whicham Valley, Silecroft, Cumbria LA18 5LT
Tel: 01229 718112 • e-mail: blackcombe@live.co.uk
Mobile: 07974 367496

Blackpool

Lancashire

Clifton Fields
Caravan Park

Situated one mile from the M55, 3.5 miles to Blackpool and 4 miles to Lytham and St Annes. Clifton Fields is a family-owned and run caravan park with a warm welcome to families and couples, offering a touring caravan field with individual hard standing and electric hook-up points, secured by an automatic barrier. Facilities include toilets, showers, elsan disposal point and a launderette.

Directions: exit M55 at Junction 4, turn left, B&Q will be on your right hand side, at the roundabout go straight on then get into the right hand lane, at the traffic lights turn right then immediately left into Peel Road. We are the second caravan park on the right hand side.

CLIFTON FIELDS CARAVAN PARK • Peel Road, Peel, Blackpool FY4 5JU
Tel: 01253 761676

www.clifton-fields.co.uk

Lancashire offers many attractions. From Clitheroe, with its castle and specialist shops, explore the beautiful Forest of Bowland in the centre of the county, wandering along the lowland riversides or tramping over the moorland hills. Follow the circular Lancashire Cycleway from north to south along sleepy roads through interesting little villages, or test your mountain biking skills in Gisburn Forest where there are trails for everyone from beginners to the highly experienced. Experience being locked in the dungeons at Lancaster Castle, on a visit to this historic centre with its cobbled streets and lively bars and restaurants. Preston, with everything from high street names to farmers' shops and markets, is the destination for shopping, as well as the National Museum of Football. Follow the Ribble Valley Food Trail to sample the wonderful produce on offer, and wherever you are look out for the panopticons, the modern sculpture installations in town and countryside.

symbols

 Holiday Parks & Centres

 Caravans for Hire

 Caravan Sites and Touring Parks

 Camping Sites

Anglesey & Gwynedd

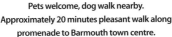

Tyddyn Isaf
Camping and Caravan Park

Lligwy Bay, Dulas, Anglesey LL70 9PQ
Tel: 01248 410203 • Fax: 01248 410667

Award-winning superior park which has been described as a 'wild life wonderland' by David Bellamy. Touring caravans and tents are catered for by the high standard of facilities – "Loo of the Year" award. The site facilities include sanitation, water, electricity, gas, shop, swings, licensed restaurant, and laundry facilities. Safe, sandy beach reached directly from the site. Golf, tennis, fishing, riding and bathing all within easy reach. Open from 1st March to 31st October.

Children welcome.
Pets by arrangement.
Tourers from £22.
Six acres for campers
from £18 per tent.
CALOR GAS 'FINALIST'
BEST TOURING PARK
IN WALES
VOTED IN TOP 100 PARKS
IN U.K. BY PRACTICAL
CARAVAN 2011

www.tyddynisaf.co.uk

Benllech

Sports and Leisure

Immediately adjacent to the site there are tennis courts and a bowling green. There is also a golf course within two miles.

A particular feature of the site is that whilst having the benefits of the village on one side, it has an attractive cliff path for walkers between the site and sea that stretches for miles. It is the intention of the local council to extend this walk right around the island.

The Site......

There are a number of flush toilet blocks together with two shower blocks. Mains water is laid in all fields, and dustbins and skips are regularly serviced. There are electric hook-ups to numerous marked-out touring caravan pitches, and hook-ups are available for tents. We have a designated family field, and one of the most popular features of the camping site is that it is split up into numerous hedged enclosures.

We do not take advanced bookings for tents and touring caravans in the main designated area, as there is usually plenty of room, although electric hook-ups cannot be guaranteed. However we do take advanced bookings for touring caravans, only a small number of which are situated within the main caravan park. During the peak season and Bank Holidays, bookings will only be taken for a minimum of a week. Seasonal tourers are welcome, and reservations can be made for these.

Organised Camps

Organised camps for schools, scouts, guides etc are welcome, and we give quotations on enquiry. Each organised camp can have its own separate field with mains water and full facilities.

GOLDEN SUNSET HOLIDAYS
BENLLECH
ANGLESEY LL74 8SW
TEL.: 01248 852345
www.goldensunsetholidays.com

Caernarfon, Criccieth

symbols

  Holiday Parks & Centres

  Caravans for Hire

  Caravan Sites and Touring Parks

  Camping Sites

Dolgellau, Snowdonia

Llwyn-Yr-Helm Farm

- Caravans, Dormobiles and tents; electric hook-ups.
- Pets welcome. • Facilities for the disabled.
- Toilet block • Laundry
- Self-catering camping lodge available.

Mrs Helen Rowlands
Llwyn-Yr-Helm Farm, Brithdir, Dolgellau LL40 2SA
Tel: 01341 450254
e-mail: info@llwynyrhelmcaravanpark.co.uk
www.llwynyrhelmcaravanpark.co.uk

Situated on a minor road half a mile off B4416 which is a loop road between A470 and A494, this is a quiet, small working farm site, four miles from Dolgellau in beautiful countryside, ideal for walking and mountain biking.

Many places of interest in the area including slate mines, narrow gauge railways, lakes and mountains and nine miles from sandy beaches.

BrynGloch

CAMPING & CARAVANNING PARK

www.campwales.co.uk

01286 650216

Nestled in a picturesque valley on the banks of the river Gwyrfai at the foot of Snowdon. Bryn Gloch boasts level all weather Super Pitches, Touring Pitches, Tent Pitches, Motorhome Pitches. Static Caravans and bunkhouse also for hire.

- **Electric Hook-ups**
- **Luxury Toilet-Shower Blocks**
- **Mother & Baby Room**
- **Disabled Facilities**
- **Fishing • Games Room**
- **Shop/Off Licence**
- **Pub & Restaurant within 1 mile**

The FHG Directory of Website Addresses

on pages 167-173 is a useful quick reference guide for holiday accommodation with e-mail and/or website details

FREE or **REDUCED RATE** entry to Holiday Visits and Attractions –
see our **READERS' OFFER VOUCHERS** on pages 175-186

Tal-y-Llyn, Trearddur Bay

Abergele, Llanrwst (Conwy Valley)

North Wales

Carmarthenshire

Argoed Meadow
Caravan and Camping Park

Beautifully situated on the banks of the River Teifi just 200 yards from the famous salmon leap and waterfalls at Cenarth, this small exclusive site is the perfect place to relax and enjoy the peace and quiet of the countryside, yet is within easy reach of the coast and other attractions.

Touring caravans, tents and camper vans catered for. Children and pets welcome. Open all year.

- Toilet and shower block with facilities for disabled visitors.
- Laundry room • BT pay phone • Electric hook-up (16 amp) • Waste disposal area

Loo of the Year Award Winners. Static Caravan available for holiday hire.

Oakwood Theme Park about 30 minutes' drive; ideal base for exploring this scenic area.

Argoed Meadow Camping & Caravan Park,
Cenarth, Newcastle Emlyn SA38 9JL
Tel: 01239 710690 • www.cenarthcampsite.co.uk

Carmarthenshire is one of the best regions for an activity or leisure break, with everything from mountain biking in the Brechfa Forest to canoeing and kayaking in the challenging stretches of the Teifi river, from walking in the foothills of the Brecon Beacons to a quiet day's fishing for sewin, salmon or trout in some remote river. The Millennium Coastal Park is one of the most popular tourist attractions in Britain, with breathtaking views of the Gower Peninsula, and a unique variety of attractions stretching from Pembrey Country Park with its acres of beautiful parkland, and one of the best beaches in the UK, as well as many excellent family activities. There are so many interesting little villages and towns to explore, with specialist shops and an endless choice of pubs, restaurants, inns and cafes to stop for something to eat and drink.

Llandysul

Ceredigion

Treddafydd Farm Caravan Site

Treddafydd, being a small site, offers a peaceful and restful holiday overlooking the beautiful Hoffnant and Penbryn valley.

All caravans have inside toilet and shower, fridge and Calor gas cookers, spacious lounge with gas heater and TV; dining area. Hot and cold water. All are fully equipped with electricity and mains water. Linen not supplied. Launderette on site, also a toilet block with two shower rooms.

Safe beach at Penbryn, one mile away (other sandy beaches nearby), cliff walks, sea and river fishing, pony rides available locally. Children are most welcome, with plenty of room for them to play. Treddafydd is a working dairy farm: cows, young calves. Children are welcome to see life on the farm. Pitches also available for tents and touring vans.

Sarnau, Llandysul SA44 6PZ • Tel: 01239 654551

Llandysul

This family-owned park is situated in the unspoilt valley leading down to Penbryn Beach. The Park is sheltered yet has views out to sea. We have modern holiday homes for hire. Tents and tourers welcome. Located in an Area of Outstanding Natural Beauty, Maes Glas is an ideal location for family holidays and also walking holidays. Short breaks available early and late season.

A warm welcome awaits you.

Mr and Mrs T. Hill, Maes Glas Caravan Park, Penbryn, Sarnau, Llandysul, Ceredigion SA44 6QE

Tel & Fax: 01239 654268

e-mail: enquiries@maesglascaravanpark.co.uk
www.maesglascaravanpark.co.uk

Pembrokeshire

Haverfordwest

❖ Brandy Brook ❖
Caravan and Camping Site

Roch, Haverfordwest SA62 6HE

This is a small, secluded site in very attractive surroundings, a quiet valley with a trout stream. The ideal situation for the true country lover. Campers welcome. Hot water/showers on site.

Car essential to get the most from your holiday. Take A487 from Haverfordwest, turn right at Roch, signposted from turning.

Pets accepted at £1.50 per night per pet. Children welcome £1.50 per night.

Rates: from £9.50 per night for one adult with tent and a car.

 Tel: 01348 840563　　❖　e-mail: a.daye@btopenworld.com

Crosskeys (Gwent)

South Wales

Cwmcarn Forest
Visitor Centre

At the foot of the spectacular seven-mile forest drive lies the Visit Wales 4* graded campsite 'Cwmcarn Forest'. Accommodation is available for up to 14 Caravans and 13 Tents (seven which are dedicated all-weather pitches), all of which have electric hook-ups. Recently arrived are our 10 camping pods, all of which have heating, lighting, electric sockets and own picnic/barbecue area. There are modern shower/toilet facilities (refurbished 2010) with chemical waste disposal, also new is a fully DDA compliant wet room.

At the entrance to the campsite is the modern Visitor Centre where you can find information on the local area, such as walks and activities. There is a well-stocked gift shop and Raven's Café serving main meals, snacks and refreshments, the perfect place to recharge your batteries.

The forest drive offers spectacular views over the surrounding countryside, with seven car parks where visitors can stop for a walk, picnic or barbecue, or let the young ones loose in the fenced adventure area at car

park three. Also on site are the world famous Twrch single track and Y Mynydd downhill mountain bike trails.

Cwmcarn Forest Visitor Centre, Cwmcarn, Crosskeys NP11 7FA
Tel: 01495 272001 • Fax: 01495 279306
e-mail: cwmcarn-vc@caerphilly.gov.uk • www.cwmcarnforest.co.uk

As well as being an ideal holiday destination in its own right Swansea Bay is a perfect base for touring the rest of South Wales. Just a short journey from the city you will find the seaside village of Mumbles and the Gower Peninsula. A great place for all sorts of watersports such as sailing and kite surfing, the beaches are perfect for surfing, for beginners and experts alike. Well known for sea fishing, there's plenty of scope for fly fishing and coarse angling as well, or you may prefer extreme hiking along Worms Head or long, leisurely strolls in the secluded coves and inlets along the coast. Cycle along one of the traffic-free routes or use up extra energy on the challenging mountain bike tracks of the Afan Forest Park. To the east follow the coastal path along the beautiful Glamorgan Heritage Coast, for views of the dramatic cliffs and the network of sand dunes at Merthyr Mawr, and golfers will enjoy a round at one of the many golf courses here, including the famous Royal Porthcawl.

Merthyr Tydfil

We are a family-run touring park on the Gower Peninsula in South Wales, approximately 16 miles from Swansea and one mile from Rhossili and the Worms Head.

Catering for touring caravans, tents and motor homes, all pitches are on level ground, well spaced around the field edges. We have a 'dog free' area and several hard standings for motor homes.

The park is set on a scenic stretch of coast, with rugged cliffs, ideal for climbing, sandy bays and secluded coves. There are endless opportunities for walking, as well as kite-flying, hang-gliding and parascending, and excellent surfing beaches.

Well-stocked on-site shop with everyday essentials, fishing bait and tackle, camping equipment, also locally made gifts and travel information.

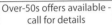

Over-50s offers available - call for details

Pitton Cross Caravan Park, Rhossili, Swansea SA3 1PT
Tel: 01792 390593 • e-mail: admin@pittoncross.co.uk
www.pittoncross.co.uk

Irresistible Orkney

Hostel, Caravan and Camping Accommodation

Warbeth Beach overlooking the Hoy Hills

Point of Ness Caravan & Camping Site, Stromness

Stromness is a small picturesque town with impressive views of the hills of Hoy.
The site is one mile from the harbour in a quiet, shoreline location.
Many leisure activities are available close by, including fishing, sea angling, golf and a swimming & fitness centre.
Contact: stromnesscashoffice@orkney.gov.uk or leisure.culture@orkney.gov.uk
www.orkney.gov.uk • Tel: 01856 850262

Birsay Outdoor Centre / Caravan & Camping Site

A new campsite located on the 3-Star hostel site in the picturesque north west of Orkney.

Hoy Centre

Four Star hostel accommodation with en suite facilities.
Ideal base for exploring Hoy's magnificent scenery and natural environment.

Rackwick Hostel

Rackwick is considered one of the most beautiful places in Orkney with towering cliffs and steep heathery hills. This cosy hostel has spectacular views over Rackwick's cliffs and beach.
For Birsay, Hoy and Rackwick contact leisure.culture@orkney.gov.uk
Tel: 01856 873535 • www.hostelsorkney.co.uk

The Pickaquoy Centre and Camping Park, Kirkwall
Tel: 01856 879900

the pickaquoy centre

A 4-Star touring park with the latest in park amenities is situated at the Pickaquoy Centre complex, an impressive leisure facility offering a range of activities for all the family.
Within walking distance of the St Magnus Cathedral and Kirkwall town centre.

e-mail: enquiries@pickaquoy.com
www.pickaquoy.co.uk

ORKNEY
ISLANDS COUNCIL

Aberdeen, Banff & Moray

Angus & Dundee

The former Pictish stronghold of Angus stretches from the sand and pebble beaches and rugged cliffs of the North Sea coast inland into the deep, narrow glens at the foothills of the Cairngorm National Park, perfect countryside for walking or for climbing, with ten 'Munros', mountains over 3000 feet, to choose from. The rivers are well known for salmon and trout fishing, alternatively sea anglers can charter a boat, or simply fish from the beach. The area is a golfers' dream, with a wide choice of courses, from classic links like Carnoustie to the heathland at Edzell in the north and parkland courses nearer the lively coastal city of Dundee. Visit the ancient port of Arbroath during the Sea Fest, celebrating its maritime heritage, and taste a traditional 'smokie'. The more recent past is commemorated in Dundee at Discovery Point, now the home of the RRS Discovery, the ship that took Captain Scott on his ill-fated journey to the Antarctic. The story of the jute industry, on which the wealth of the city was built, is retold at the Verdant Works, but this city formerly associated with jute, jam and journalism now looks to the future too at the Sensation Science Centre, where everyone can experiment with interactive exhibits involving robotics, cybernetics and even keyhole surgery.

Eastmill Caravan Park
Brechin, Angus DD9 7EL

Beautifully situated on flat grassy site along the River South Esk, within easy access of scenic Angus Glens, local walks and 10 miles from sandy east coast beaches; midway between Dundee and Aberdeen.

Shop, gas supplies, shower block, laundry and hook-ups on site; licensed premises nearby.

Six-berth caravans with mains services available to rent.

Facilities for tourers, caravanettes and tents. Dogs welcome.

Open April to October.

Telephone: 01356 625206
(out of season 01356 622487)
Fax: 01356 623356

Argyll & Bute

Argyll & Bute is a wonderfully unspoilt area, historically the birthplace of Scotland and home to a wealth of fascinating wildlife. Here you may be lucky enough to catch a glimpse of an eagle, a wildcat or an osprey, whales, dolphin, seals, or even a giant octopus. At every step the sea fringed landscape is steeped in history, from prehistoric sculpture at Kilmartin and Knapdale, standing stone circles and Bronze Age cup-and-ring engravings, to the elegant ducal home of the once feared Clan Campbell. On the upper reaches of Loch Caolisport can be found St Columba's Cave, and more recent times are illustrated at the Auchindrain Highland Township south of Inveraray, a friendly little town with plenty to see, including the Jail, Wildlife Park and Maritime Museum. Bute is the most accessible of the west coast islands, and Rothesay is its main town. Here find out about the island at the Discovery Centre, explore the dungeons and grand hall of Rothesay Castle, and visit the Victorian gothic splendour of Mount Stuart nearby.

ROSNEATH CASTLE PARK
SO NEAR... YET SO FAR AWAY

Rosneath Castle Park has everything to offer if you are looking for a relaxing holiday. No more than an hour's drive from Glasgow, the 57 acres that the park occupies along the shore of Gareloch offer the perfect opportunity to relax and discover another world, and another you.

Thistle Awarded Luxury Self-Catering Holiday Homes with superb views. In a beautiful setting with first class facilities including an adventure playground, boat house, fun club, restaurant and bar, there's no end to the reasons why you would 'wish you were here'.

Rosneath Castle Park, Rosneath,
Near Helensburgh, Argyll G84 0QS
Tel: (01436) 831208
Fax: (01436) 831978
enquiries@rosneathcastle.demon.co.uk
www.rosneathcastle.co.uk

CAOLASNACON
Caravan & Camping Park, Kinlochleven PH50 4RJ

There are 20 static six-berth caravans for holiday hire on this lovely site with breathtaking mountain scenery on the edge of Loch Leven — an ideal touring centre.

Caravans have electric lighting, Calor gas cookers
and heaters, toilet, shower, fridge and TV/DVD.
Toilet block with hot water,
free showers and laundry facilities.
Children are welcome and pets allowed.
Milk and gas available on site; shops three miles.
Sea loch fishing, hill walking and boating.
Open from April to October.

For details contact Mrs Patsy Cameron
Tel: 01855 831279
e-mail: enquiry@kinlochlevencaravans.com
www.kinlochlevencaravans.com

Port Ban Holiday Park

Kilberry, Tarbert, Argyll PA29 6YD
Tel: 01880 770224
www.portban.com
e-mail: portban@aol.com

Beautiful, remote, secluded, coastal park enjoying fantastic sunsets over the Paps of Jura. Many sports facilities including Games Hall, Putting Green, Football Pitch, Tennis Court, Crazy Golf, Bowling Green and also Bikes for Hire.
Sandy beaches and rock pools.
Organised events during school holidays including children's club, sports competitions and ceilidhs.

Ideal for wildlife enthusiasts – dolphins, seals, birds of prey, wildflowers etc.
Shop selling gifts and basic groceries.
Cafe selling snacks, homemade cakes and freshly ground coffees.
Standard and Luxury caravans for hire from £200 -£455 per week.

Pitches available for tourers and Tents from £8/night.
Reduced rates for Senior Citizens outside school holidays.

Christian Fellowship available and Services held during School Holidays.

Lochranza

Ayrshire & Arran

LOCHRANZA
CARAVAN & CAMPING SITE

A quiet site on the delightful Isle of Arran, close to
Arran Distillery and Kintyre ferry.
Touring tents, motorhomes and caravans welcome.
Facilities include: hot showers, electric hook-ups, launderette,
chemical disposal point and 9 hole golf.
Lots of walking, cycling and wildlife in the area.
Lochranza Campsite, Isle of Arran KA27 8HL
Tel: 01770 830273 • www.arran-campsite.com

symbols

☼	*Holiday Parks & Centres*
🚐	*Caravans for Hire*
Ⓢ	*Caravan Sites and Touring Parks*
⋀	*Camping Sites*

Castle Douglas

Dumfries & Galloway

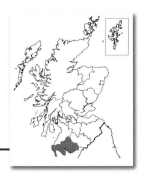

Silvercraigs Caravan & Camping Site is an elevated site overlooking the town of Kirkcudbright providing panoramic views over the Solway Coast & Twynholm Hills. The site can accommodate pitches for 37 caravans and 13 tents. Electric hook-ups and laundry facilities are available. Open Easter to October.

Silvercraigs Caravan & Camping Site

Kirkcudbright DG6 4BT Tel: 07824528482
email: Silvercraigs.caravan@dumgal.gov.uk
www.dumgal.gov.uk

At the lower end of the site is a children's play area. Sandy beaches are just a few miles away. Kirkcudbright, famous as an artists' colony, is a short walk down from the site, with museum, art galleries, swimming pool, tennis courts, golf, bowling and wildlife park as well as extensive summer festivities.

Dumfries & Galloway combines high moorland and sheltered glens, forests, sandy beaches, crags, cliffs and rocky shores, presenting abundant opportunities for hill walking, rambling, fishing for salmon and sea trout, cycling, mountain biking, off-road driving, horse riding, pony trekking and bird watching. Catch a glimpse of a red kite soaring above, or a wild goat or red squirrel in the 300 square miles of the Galloway Forest Park or hunt for sea life in a rocky coastal pool. Golfers can choose from 30 courses, whether the challenging links at Southerness or a local course with spectacular views. Warmed by the influence of the Gulf Stream, touring in this quiet corner of south west Scotland is a pleasure, visiting the dozens of interesting castles, gardens, museums and historic sites. In addition a never-ending succession of music festivals, ceilidhs, village fairs, country dances, classical music concerts and children's entertainment guarantees plenty of scope for enjoyment.

East Calder

Edinburgh & Lothians

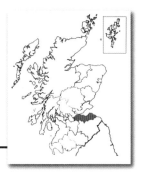

CARAVAN PARK

A family-run touring park set in countryside, just west of Edinburgh, with excellent facilities and lovely walks to the Union Canal and Almondell Country Park. Ideal for visiting Edinburgh, with nearby Park and Ride, Royal Highland Showground and the Falkirk Wheel, or touring with excellent access to all routes for travelling further afield. Or try our timbertents, a warm and dry alternative to camping. We are an ideal stop-over on your way north or south, or stay awhile, you will be most welcome.

Linwater Caravan Park, West Clifton, East Calder, West Lothian EH53 0HT • Tel: 0131 333 3326
queries@linwater.co.uk • www.linwater.co.uk

Visitors to Edinburgh, Scotland's capital, and the surrounding area, the Lothians, will find a wide range of attractions offering something for all ages and interests. Heritage is paramount, with historic and royal connections through the ages centred on Edinburgh Castle, down the Royal Mile to the Palace of Holyroodhouse, and its new neighbour, the Scottish Parliament building. Stroll through the Georgian New Town, browsing through some of the many shops on the way, or a wander through the Royal Botanic Gardens. Imagine sailing on the Royal Yacht Britannia, now berthed at Leith, or travel on a journey with our planet through time and space at Our Dynamic Earth. The Edinburgh Festival in August is part of the city's tradition and visitors flock to enjoy the performing arts, theatre, ballet, cinema and music, and of course "The Tattoo" itself. At the Festival Fringe there is a wide variety of shows and impromptu acts, and jazz and book festivals too.

Highlands

Apart from the stunning scenery, the major attraction of The Scottish Highlands is that there is so much to see and do, whatever the season. Stretching from Fort William in the south, to Wick in the far north, there is a wealth of visitor attractions and facilities. Loch Ness, home of the legendary monster, is perhaps the most famous of these attractions and the Visitor Centre also provides a variety of souvenirs, including kilts and whisky. Make sure that a visit to the bustling Highland capital city of Inverness is on your itinerary, and don't miss Fort William in the Western Highlands, a busy town with a wide range of shops and services, pubs, restaurants and Scottish entertainment. The North West Highlands is home to the nation's first Geopark, underlining the importance of the area's geological past. John O'Groats is, of course, the ultimate destination of most travellers as it was for the Norsemen centuries ago, whose heritage is preserved in the Northlands Viking Centre at Auckengill.

Almost a botanical garden, Linnhe is recognised as one of the best and most beautiful Lochside parks in Britain. Magnificent gardens contrast with the wild, dramatic scenery of Loch Eil and the

 mountains beyond. Superb amenities, launderette, shop & bakery, and free fishing on private shoreline with its own jetty all help give Linnhe its Five Star grading. Linnhe Lochside Holidays is ideally situated for day trips with Oban, Skye, Mull, Inverness and the Cairngorms all within easy driving distance.

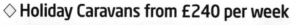

◇ **Holiday Caravans from £240 per week**
◇ **Touring pitches from £16 per night**
◇ **Tent pitches from £12 per night**
◇ **Pets welcome**
◇ **Tourer playground, pet exercise area**
◇ **Motorhome waste and water facilities**
◇ **Recycling on park**
◇ **Colour brochure sent with pleasure.**

www.linnhe-lochside-holidays.co.uk/brochure
Tel: 01397 772 376 to check availability

Hillhead Caravans
Achmelvich

Excellent self-catering accommodation at the beautiful white, safe, sandy beach of Achmelvich, near Lochinver in North West Scotland, one of the country's beauty spots. Ideal for family holidays. Clean, modern, 6-berth, fully serviced caravans to let, 150 metres from the beach.

Our accommodation and area are perfect for country lovers and a good centre for hillwalking, photography, cycling, climbing, caving, geology, swimming, bird-watching, touring, fishing, sailing – or just relaxing with a good book! Open late March to late October.

Details from Durrant and Maysie Macleod
Hillhead Caravans, Lochinver IV27 4JA
Tel: 01571 844206
e-mail:info@lochinverholidays.co.uk

symbols

☼	*Holiday Parks & Centres*
	Caravans for Hire
	Caravan Sites and Touring Parks
Ⓐ	*Camping Sites*

Abington

Lanarkshire

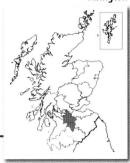

Luxury holiday homes for hire on caravan park set in peaceful, unspoilt countryside with beautiful views of the Clyde valley. Good for walking, cycling, fishing, golf and touring the area. Near to Moffat, Biggar, Edinburgh, Glasgow and Scottish Borders.

Fully equipped holiday home including microwave, TV/DVD and with double glazing and central heating.

En suite shower room, lounge, dining area, kitchen, twin and double bedrooms. Bedding and towels can be provided at an extra cost.

Easy access, just five minutes from J13 of the M74 and a short walk from the village shop.

£190 to £360 per week.

Abington, South Lanarkshire ML12 6RW   Tel: 01864 502808
e-mail: info@mountviewcaravanpark.co.uk • www.mountviewcaravanpark.co.uk

Perth & Kinross

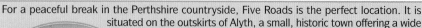

Largo Leisure Parks

For Living Life to the Full

Our holiday parks are ideally suited for those seeking a tranquil retreat with beautiful scenery, whilst enjoying the many and varied attractions of the Kingdom of Fife and Perthshire areas of Scotland.

Holiday homes are perfect for getting away from it all. Our parks offer the atmosphere to relax and enjoy the long holiday or short break.

Sauchope Links Park is situated on the shoreline, near the eastern most tip of Fife in a beautiful, unspoilt position close to the historic town of Crail. This award winning park with stunning views makes the perfect holiday destination.

Letham Feus Park is situated only 3 miles from Lundin Links with its championship golf course and beautiful sandy beach. The park is blessed with breathtaking views over the Forth Estuary to the South and beautiful woodland to the north. Letham Feus is the perfect place to take that well earned break.

Braidhaugh Park is situated on the banks of the River Earn amid the scenic surroundings of Crieff. The park is an ideal base from which to explore not only the beautiful surroundings of Perthshire, but also the magnificent scenic grandeur of Central Scotland.

Loch Tay Highland Lodges Holiday Park is beautifully situated on a well established 140 acre Highland Estate nestling on the shores of Loch Tay in Perthshire. It is the perfect all year round holiday destination for those who love pure relaxation or for those energetic types who love the great outdoors.

Sauchope Links Holiday Park, Crail, Fife KY10 3XJ
Tel: 01333 450 460 info@sauchope.co.uk

Letham Feus Holiday Park, Cupar Rd by Lundin Links KY8 5NT
Tel: 01333 351 900 info@lethamfeus.co.uk

Braidhaugh Holiday Park, South Bridgend, Crieff PH7 4DH
Tel: 01764 652951 info@braidhaugh.co.uk

Loch Tay Highland Lodges, Milton Morenish Estate by Killin,
Perthshire FK21 8TY Tel: 01567 820323
info@lochtay-vacations.co.uk www.lochtay-vacations.co.uk

www.largoleisure.co.uk

Pitlochry, Perthshire PH16 5NA

Our family-run caravan park lies on the banks of the River Tummel, in the heart of the country, yet within less than ten minutes walking distance of Pitlochry town centre. With open views of the Tummel Valley and the surrounding hills, the site is level, well-drained and with tarmac roads all round.

We have static vans for hire and provide pitches for mobile caravans, motorhomes and tents.

We also offer an excellent range of on-site facilities for our guests, as well as leisure activities including trout and salmon fishing. Open March to October.

Our static vans all have a comfortable lounge area with ample storage space, gas heater, colour television

and DVD player. Fully fitted kitchen area and shower, toilet, wash-hand basin. Duvets and pillows provided, the only item that visitors are required to bring is their own bed linen.

170 pitches available for touring vans and motorhomes. Shower and washroom facilities available. Limited spaces for small tents. Caravans £300-£600 per week; pitches from £18 per night.

Trout and salmon fishing, boating on Loch Faskally, sailing on Loch Tummel, tennis, bowling, golfing, putting, hillwalking and pony trekking all available.

Milton of Fonab Caravan Park
Tel: 01796 472882 • Fax: 01796 474363
e-mail: info@fonab.co.uk • www.fonab.co.uk

Aberfoyle

Stirling & The Trossachs

At the heart of Scotland, Stirling, Loch Lomond and the Trossachs combines history and scenic beauty, and endless opportunities for walking, cycling and boating, all within an hour of Edinburgh and Glasgow. Stirling Castle, magnificently restored to tell the story of this former seat of Scottish monarchs, provides a panoramic view from Ben Lomond across the Trossachs and over Bannockburn and other battlegrounds so important in Scotland's history. Explore the wild glens and sparkling lochs in Loch Lomond and The Trossachs National Park, and perhaps take a steamer trip down Loch Katrine. Whatever your fitness, there are walks suitable for everyone, cycle routes, challenging mountain bike trails, golf and wildlife. The amazing Falkirk Wheel linking the Forth and Clyde and Union Canals is a sight and experience not to be missed, while villages and small towns such as Drymen, Killearn, Fintry and Kippen offer hospitality and interesting outings less than an hour from Glasgow, yet feels worlds apart from the bustle of city life.

Scottish Islands

Isle of Barra
Static Caravan for Hire

- One double bedroom
- Two rooms with single beds in each
- Living room • Kitchen with gas cooker
- Instant running hot and cold water • Gas heater
- Shower room • WC • Bed linen, utensils etc. provided.

**Located at 12 Eoligarry, Isle of Barra HS9 5YD
Price from £200 per week.**

**Contact: Mr D. Maclean
Tel: 01871 890 723 or 0141 954 2101
email: barraaccommodation@hotmail.com**

So many islands are waiting to be visited off the Scottish mainland, each with a mystery and magic of its own. To the north lie the Orkney and Shetland Isles, with their strong connections to the Vikings whose influence is still seen and heard today. To the west, exposed to the Atlantic, lie the Inner and Outer Hebrides, including the islands of Skye, Islay, Mull and Tiree, Lewis, Harris and Barra, each with its own culture, traditions and heritage. Everywhere there's evidence of settlement going back to prehistoric times, including awe-inspiring standing stones and circles and chambered cairns. Some islands have mountains to climb, but most are low-lying, ideal for exploring on foot and for cycling and bird watching, while the Atlantic waves have proved a great attraction to surfers from all over the world.

Kirkwall

Lauragh

Ireland

Creveen Lodge

Immaculately run small hill farm overlooking Kenmare Bay in a striking area of County Kerry. Reception is found at the Lodge, which also offers guests a comfortable sitting room, while a separate block has well-equipped and immaculately maintained toilets and showers, plus a communal room with a large fridge, freezer and ironing facilities. The park is carefully tended, with bins and picnic tables informally placed, plus a children's play area with slides and swings.

There are 20 pitches in total, 16 for tents and 4 for caravans, with an area of hardstanding for motor caravans. Electrical connections are available. Fishing, bicycle hire, water sports and horse riding available nearby. SAE please, for replies.

Mrs M. Moriarty, Creveen Lodge, Healy Pass Road, Lauragh
00 353 64 66 83131
e-mail: info@creveenlodge.com • www.creveenlodge.com

symbols

 Holiday Parks & Centres

 Caravans for Hire

 Caravan Sites and Touring Parks

 Camping Sites

Please note...

All the information in this book is given in good faith in the belief that it is correct.
However, the publishers cannot guarantee the facts given in these pages, neither are they
responsible for changes in policy, ownership or terms that may take place after the date of going to
press. Readers should always satisfy themselves that the facilities they require
are available and that the terms, if quoted, still apply.

Antrim

Six Mile Water Caravan Park

NITB
★★★★★

Lough Road, Antrim BT41 4DG

Situated at Antrim Lough Shore Park, on the tranquil and scenic shores of Lough Neagh, within easy walking distance of Antrim town and Antrim Forum Leisure Complex. The park's central location, coupled with its close proximity to Larne and Belfast harbours, make it an ideal base for touring not only the Borough of Antrim but all of Northern Ireland. The park accommodates touring caravans, motorhomes and tents.

Electric hook-up for 37 pitches. 8 camping sites. Toilet and shower block. Disabled shower room. Fully equipped laundry and dishwashing facilities. TV lounge. Games room. Recycling facilities. Licensed cafe. Dogs allowed. Group discount on request. Advance booking advisable. Open February to November. Bookings can be made online, website or by phone.

Tel: 028 9446 4963
e-mail:sixmilewater@antrim.gov.uk
www.antrim.gov.uk/caravanpark

Six Mile Water
Caravan Park

DIRECTORY OF WEBSITE AND E-MAIL ADDRESSES

A quick-reference guide to holiday accommodation with an e-mail address and/or website, conveniently arranged by country and county, with full contact details.

•LONDON

Hotel
Athena Hotel, 110-114 Sussex Gardens, Hyde Park, LONDON W2 1UA
Tel: 020 7706 3866
• e-mail: stay@athenahotellondon.co.uk
• website: www.athenahotel.co.uk

•BERKSHIRE

Touring Campsite
Wellington Country Park, Odiham Road, Riseley, Near READING, Berkshire RG7 1SP
Tel : 0118 932 6444
• e-mail: info@wellington-country-park.co.uk
• website: www.wellington-country-park.co.uk

•CHESHIRE

Farmhouse B & B
Astle Farm East, Chelford, MACCLESFIELD, Cheshire SK10 4TA
Tel: 01625 861270
• e-mail: stubg@aol.com
• website: www.astlefarmeast.co.uk

•CORNWALL

Self-Catering
Penrose Burden Holiday Cottages, St Breward, BODMIN, Cornwall PL30 4LZ
Tel : 01208 850277
• website: www.penroseburden.co.uk

Self-Catering / Caravan
Mrs A. E. Moore, Hollyvagg Farm, Lewannick, LAUNCESTON, Cornwall PL15 7QH
Tel: 01566 782309
• website: www.hollyvaggfarm.co.uk

Self- Catering
Mr Lowman, Cutkive Wood Holiday Lodges, St Ive, LISKEARD, Cornwall PL14 3ND
Tel: 01579 362216
• e-mail: holidays@cutkivewood.co.uk
• website: www.cutkivewood.co.uk

Self-Catering
Butterdon Mill Holiday Homes, Merrymeet, LISKEARD, Cornwall PL14 3LS
Tel: 01579 342636
• e-mail: butterdonmill@btconnect.com
• website: www.bmhh.co.uk

Caravan / Camping
Quarryfield Caravan & Camping Park, Crantock, NEWQUAY, Cornwall
Contact: Mrs A Winn, Tretherras, Newquay, Cornwall TR7 2RE
Tel: 01637 872792
• e-mails:
quarryfield@crantockcaravans.orangehome.co.uk
info@quarryfield.co.uk
• website: www.quarryfield.co.uk

B&B
Bolankan Cottage B & B, Crows-an-Wra, St Buryan, PENZANCE, Cornwall TR19 6HU
Tel: 01736 810168
• e-mail: bolankancottage@talktalk.net
• website: www.bolankan-cottage.co.uk

Caravan / Camping
Globe Vale Holiday Park, Radnor, REDRUTH, Cornwall TR16 4BH
Tel: 01209 891183
• e-mail: info@globevale.co.uk
• website: www.globevale.co.uk

Guest House
Mr S Hope, Dalswinton House, ST MAWGAN-IN-PYDAR, Cornwall TR8 4EZ
Tel: 01637 860385
• e-mail: dalswintonhouse@btconnect.com
• website: www.dalswinton.com

Self-Catering
Maymear Cottage, ST TUDY
Contact: Ruth Reeves, Polstraul, Trewalder,
Delabole, Cornwall PL33 9ET
Tel: 01840 213120
• e-mail: ruth.reeves@hotmail.co.uk
• website: www.maymear.co.uk

Self-Catering
The Garden House, Port Isaac, Near
WADEBRIDGE, Cornwall
Contact: Mr D Oldham, Trevella,
Treveighan, St Teath, Cornwall PL30 3JN
Tel: 01208 850529
• e-mail: david.trevella@btconnect.com
• website: www.trevellacornwall.co.uk

• CUMBRIA

Caravan Park
Greenhowe Caravan Park, Great Langdale,
AMBLESIDE, Cumbria LA22 9JU
Tel: 015394 37231
• e-mail: enquiries@greenhowe.com
• website: www.greenhowe.com

B&B
Smallwood House, Compston Road,
AMBLESIDE, Cumbria LA22 9DH
Tel: 015394 32330
• website: www.smallwoodhotel.co.uk

Self-Catering
Mrs Almond, Irton House Farm, Isel, Near
KESWICK, Cumbria CA13 9ST
Tel: 017687 76380
• e-mail: joan@irtonhousefarm.co.uk
• website: www.irtonhousefarm.com

Self-Catering
Mr D Williamson, Derwent Water Marina,
Portinscale, KESWICK, Cumbria CA12 5RF
Tel: 017687 72912
• e-mail: info@derwentwatermarina.co.uk
• website: www.derwentwatermarina.co.uk

Self-Catering
Mrs S.J. Bottom, Crossfield Cottages,
KIRKOSWALD, Penrith, Cumbria CA10 1EU
Tel: 01768 898711
• e-mail: info@crossfieldcottages.co.uk
• website: www.crossfieldcottages.co.uk

• DERBYSHIRE

Self-Catering Holiday Cottages
Mark Redfern, Paddock House Farm Holiday
Cottages, Peak District National Park,
Alstonefield, ASHBOURNE, Derbyshire
DE6 2FT
Tel: 01335 310282 / 07977 569618
• e-mail: info@paddockhousefarm.co.uk
• website: www.paddockhousefarm.co.uk

Caravan
Golden Valley Caravan Park, Coach Road,
RIPLEY, Derbyshire DE55 4ES
Tel: 01773 513881
• e-mail:
enquiries@goldenvalleycaravanpark.co.uk
• website: www.goldenvalleycaravanpark.co.uk

• DEVON

Self-Catering
Mrs A. Bell, Wooder Manor, Widercombe-in-
the-Moor, Near ASHBURTON, Devon
TQ13 7TR
Tel: 01364 621391
• website: www.woodermanor.com

Hotel
Fairwater Head Hotel, Hawkchurch, Near
AXMINSTER, Devon EX13 5TX
Tel: 01297 678349
• e-mail: stay@fairwaterheadhotel.co.uk
• website: www.fairwaterheadhotel.co.uk

Self-Catering / B&B
Lake House Cottages and B&B, Lake
Villa, BRADWORTHY, Devon EX22 7SQ
Tel : 01409 241962
• email: lesley@lakevilla.co.uk
• website: www.lakevilla.co.uk

Self-Catering
Linda & Jim Watt, Northcote Manor
Farm Holiday Cottages, Kentisbury,
COMBE MARTIN, Devon EX31 4NB
Tel: 01271 882376
• e-mail: info@northcotemanorfarm.co.uk
• website: www.northcotemanorfarm.co.uk

Self-Catering
G Davidson Richmond, Clooneavin,
Clooneavin Path, LYNMOUTH, Devon
EX35 6EE
Tel: 01598 753334
• e-mail: relax@clooneavinholidays.co.uk
• website: www.clooneavinholidays.co.uk

FHG Guides

Guest House
Mr. & Mrs D. Fitzgerald, Beaumont, Castle
Hill, SEATON, Devon EX12 2QW
Tel: 01297 20832
• e-mail: **beaumont.seaton@talktalk.net**
• website:
www.smoothhound.co.uk/hotels/beaumon1.html

Caravans / Camping
Salcombe Regis Camping & Caravan
Park, SIDMOUTH, Devon EX10 0JH
Tel: 01395 514303
• e-mail: **contact@salcombe-regis.co.uk**
• website: **www.salcombe-regis.co.uk**

Self-Catering / Camping
Dartmoor Country Holidays, Magpie Leisure
Park, Bedford Bridge, Horrabridge,
Yelverton, TAVISTOCK, Devon PL20 7RY
Tel: 01822 852651
• website: **www.dartmoorcountryholidays.co.uk**

Caravan & Camping
North Morte Farm Caravan & Camping Park,
Mortehoe, WOOLACOMBE, Devon EX34 7EG
Tel: 01271 870381
• e-mail: **info@northmortefarm.co.uk**
• website: **www.northmortefarm.co.uk**

•DORSET

Self-Catering
C. Hammond, Stourcliffe Court, 56
Stourcliffe Avenue, Southbourne,
BOURNEMOUTH, Dorset BH6 3PX
Tel: 01202 420698
• e-mail: **rjhammond1@hotmail.co.uk**
• website: **www.stourcliffecourt.co.uk**

Self-Catering Cottage / Farmhouse B & B
Mrs S. E. Norman, Frogmore Farm,
Chideock, BRIDPORT, Dorset DT6 6HT
Tel: 01308 456159
• e-mail: **bookings@frogmorefarm.com**
• website: **www.frogmorefarm.com**

B&B
Nethercroft, Winterbourne Abbas,
DORCHESTER, Dorset DT2 9LU
Tel: 01305 889337
• e-mail: **val.bradbeer@btconnect.com**
• website: **www.nethercroft.com**

Farmhouse B&B / Caravan & Camping
Luckford Wood Farmhouse, Church
Street, East Stoke, Wareham, Near
LULWORTH, Dorset BH20 6AW
Tel: 01929 463098 / 07888 719002
• e-mail: **luckfordleisure@hotmail.co.uk**
• website: **www.luckfordleisure.co.uk**

Self-Catering
Westover Farm Cottages, Wootton Fitzpaine,
Near LYME REGIS, Dorset DT6 6NE
Tel: 01297 560451/07979 265064
• e-mail: **wfcottages@aol.com**
• website: **www.westoverfarmcottages.co.uk**

Hotel
The Knoll House, STUDLAND BAY,
Dorset BH19 3AH
Tel: 01929 450450
• e-mail: **info@knollhouse.co.uk**
• website: **www.knollhouse.co.uk**

Inn B&B
The White Swan, The Square, 31 High
Street, SWANAGE BN19 2LJ
Tel: 01929 423804
• e-mail: **info@whiteswanswanage.co.uk**
• website: **www.whiteswanswanage.co.uk**

•GLOUCESTERSHIRE

Self-Catering
Two Springbank, 37 Hopton Road, Cam,
DURSLEY, Gloucs GL11 5PD
Contact: Mrs F A Jones, 32 Everlands, Cam,
Dursley, Gloucs G11 5NL
Tel: 01453 543047
• e-mail: **info@twospringbank.co.uk**
• website: **www.twospringbank.co.uk**

B & B
Mrs A Rhoton, Hyde Crest, Cirencester Road,
Minchinhampton, STROUD, Gloucs GL6 8PE
Tel: 01453 731631
• e-mail: **stay@hydecrest.co.uk**
• website: **www.hydecrest.co.uk**

•HAMPSHIRE

Holiday Park
Downton Holiday Park, Shorefield Road,
Milford-on-Sea, LYMINGTON, Hampshire
SO41 0LH
Tel: 01425 476131 / 01590 642515
• e-mail: **info@downtonholidaypark.co.uk**
• website: **www.downtonholidaypark.co.uk**

•LANCASHIRE

Guest House
Parr Hall Farm, Parr Lane, Eccleston,
Chorley, PRESTON, Lancs PR7 5SL
Tel: 01257 451917
• e-mail: **enquiries@parrhallfarm.com**
• website: **www.parrhallfarm.com**

•NORFOLK

Self-catering
Scarning Dale, Dale Road, Scarning,
DEREHAM, Norfolk NR19 2QN
Tel: 01362 687269
• e-mail: jean@scarningdale.co.uk
• website: www.scarningdale.co.uk

Holiday Park
Waveney Valley Holiday Park, Airstation
Lane, Rushall, DISS, Norfolk IP21 4QF
Tel: 01379 741228
• e-mail: waveneyvalleyhp@aol.com
• website: www.caravanparksnorfolk.co.uk

Self-Catering
Blue Riband Holidays, HEMSBY,
Great Yarmouth, Norfolk NR29 4HA
Tel: 01493 730445
• websites: www.blueribandrolidays.co.uk
      www.parklandshemsby.co.uk

Self-Catering
Winterton Valley Holidays, Edward Road,
WINTERTON-ON-SEA, Norfolk NR29 4BX
Contact:15 Kingston Avenue, Caister-on-
Sea, Norfolk NR30 5ET
Tel: 01493 377175
• e-mail: info@wintertonvalleyholidays.co.uk
• website: www.wintertonvalleyholidays.co.uk

•NOTTINGHAMSHIRE

Caravan & Camping Park
Orchard Park, Marnham Road, Tuxford,
NEWARK, Nottinghamshire NG22 0PY
Tel: 01777 870228
• e-mail: info@orchardcaravanpark.co.uk
• website: www.orchardcaravanpark.co.uk

•OXFORDSHIRE

B&B
Middle Fell, Moreton Road, Aston Upthorpe,
DIDCOT, Oxfordshire OX11 9ER
Tel: 01235 850207
• e-mail: middlefell@ic24.net
• website: www.middlefell.co.uk

B & B / Guest House
June Collier, Colliers B&B, 55 Nethercote
Road, Tackley, KIDLINGTON, Oxfordshire
OX5 3AT
Tel: 01869 331255 / 07790 338225
• e-mail: junecollier@btinternet.com
• website: www.colliersbnb.co.uk

•SHROPSHIRE

Self-Catering
Clive & Cynthia Prior, Mocktree Barns
Holiday Cottages, Leintwardine, LUDLOW,
Shropshire SY7 0LY
Tel: 01547 540441
• e-mail: mocktreebarns@care4free.net
• website: www.mocktreeholidays.co.uk

Self-Catering
Jane Cronin, Sutton Court Farm Cottages,
Sutton Court Farm, Little Sutton, LUDLOW,
Shropshire SY8 2AJ
Tel: 01584 861305
• e-mail: enquiries@suttoncourtfarm.co.uk
• website: www.suttoncourtfarm.co.uk

•SOMERSET

Farm / Guest House / Self-Catering
Jackie Bishop, Toghill House Farm, Freezing
Hill, Wick, Near BATH, Somerset BS30 5RT
Tel: 01225 891261
• e-mail:
accommodation@toghillhousefarm.co.uk
• website: www.toghillhousefarm.co.uk

Self-Catering
Westward Rise Holiday Park, South Road,
BREAN, Burnham-on-Sea, Somerset TA8 2RD
Tel: 01278 751310
• e-mail: info@westwardrise.com
• website: www.westwardrise.com

Self-Catering / Holiday Park / Touring Pitches
James Randle, St Audries Bay Holiday Club,
West Quantoxhead, MINEHEAD, Somerset
TA4 4DY
Tel: 01984 632515
• e-mail: info@staudriesbay.co.uk
• website: www.staudriesbay.co.uk

Farm / Guest House
G. Clark, Yew Tree Farm, THEALE,
Near Wedmore, Somerset BS28 4SN
Tel: 01934 712475
• e-mail: enquiries@yewtreefarmbandb.co.uk
• website: www.yewtreefarmbandb.co.uk

•SUFFOLK

Self-Catering
Kessingland Cottages, Rider Haggard Lane,
KESSINGLAND, Suffolk.
Contact: S. Mahmood, 156 Bromley Road,
Beckenham, Kent BR3 6PG
Tel: 020 8650 0539
• e-mail: jeeptrek@kjti.co.uk
• website: www.k-cottage.co.uk

Holiday Park
Broadland Holiday Village, Oulton
Broad, LOWESTOFT, Suffolk NR33 9JY
Tel: 01502 573033
• e-mail: info@broadlandvillage.co.uk
• website: www.broadlandvillage.co.uk

•EAST SUSSEX

Hotel
Grand Hotel, 1 Grand Parade, St Leonards,
HASTINGS, East Sussex TN37 6AQ
Tel: 01424 428510
• e-mail: info@grandhotelhastings.co.uk
• website: www.grandhotelhastings.co.uk

Self-Catering
"Pekes", CHIDDINGLY, East Sussex
Contact: Eva Morris, 124 Elm Park
Mansions, Park Walk, London SW10 0AR
Tel: 020 7352 8088
• e-mail: pekes.afa@virgin.net
• website: www.pekesmanor.com

Guest House / Self-Catering
Longleys Farm Cottage, Harebeating Lane,
HAILSHAM, East Sussex BN27 1ER
Tel: 01323 841227
• website: www.longleysfarmcottage.co.uk

• WEST SUSSEX

Guest Accommodation
St Andrews Lodge, Chichester Road,
SELSEY, West Sussex PO20 0LX
Tel: 01243 606899
• e-mail: info@standrewslodge.co.uk
• website: www.standrewslodge.co.uk

•WARWICKSHIRE

Guest House
John & Julia Downie, Holly Tree
Cottage, Pathlow, STRATFORD-UPON-
AVON, Warwickshire CV37 0ES
Tel: 01789 204461
• e-mail: john@hollytree-cottage.co.uk
• website: www.hollytree-cottage.co.uk

•NORTH YORKSHIRE

Self-Catering
Rudding Holiday Park, Follifoot,
HARROGATE, North Yorkshire HG3 1JH
Tel: 01423 870439
• e-mail: stay@ruddingpark.com
• website: www.ruddingholidaypark.co.uk

Self-Catering
Southfield Farm Holiday Cottages,
Darley, HARROGATE, North Yorkshire
HG3 2PR
Tel: 01423 780258
• e-mail: info@southfieldcottages.co.uk
• website: www.southfieldcottages.co.uk

Farmhouse B & B
Mrs Julie Clarke, Middle Farm, Woodale,
Coverdale, LEYBURN, North Yorkshire
DL8 4TY
Tel: 01969 640271
• e-mail: j-a-clarke@hotmail.co.uk
• www.yorkshirenet.co.uk/stayat/middlefarm/
index.htm

Self-Catering
2 Hollies Cottages, Stainforth, SETTLE,
N.Yorkshire
Contact : Bridge Cottage, Stainforth,
Near Settle BD24 9PG
Tel: 01729 822649
• e-mail: vivmills30@hotmail.com
• website: www.stainforth-holiday-cottage-
settle.co.uk

Self-Catering
York Lakeside Lodges Ltd, Moor Lane,
YORK, North Yorkshire YO24 2QU
Tel: 01904 702346
• e-mail: neil@yorklakesidelodges.co.uk
• website: www.yorklakesidelodges.co.uk

Bestselling holiday accommodation guides for over 65 years

WALES

•ANGLESEY & GWYNEDD

Self-Catering Chalet
Chalet at Glan Gwna Holiday Park, Caethro, CAERNARFON, Gwynedd
Contact: Mr H A Jones, 12 Lon Isaf, Menai Bridge, Anglesey LL59 5LN
Tel: 01248 712045
• e-mail: hajones@northwales-chalet.co.uk
• website: www.northwales-chalet.co.uk

Self-Catering
Parc Wernol, Chwilog Fawr, Chwilog, PWLLHELI, Criccieth, Gwynedd LL53 6SW
Tel: 01766 810506
• e-mail: catherine@wernol.co.uk
• website: www.wernol.co.uk

• PEMBROKESHIRE

Self-Catering
Llanteglos Estate, Llanteg, Near AMROTH, Pembs SA67 8PU
• e-mail: llanteglosestate@supanet.com
• website: www.llanteglos-estate.com

Self-Catering
Timberhill Farm, BROAD HAVEN, Pembrokeshire SA62 3LZ
Contact: Mrs L Ashton, 10 St Leonards Road, Thames Ditton, Surrey KT7 0RJ
Tel: 02083 986349
• e-mail: lejash@aol.com
• website: www.33timberhill.co

Self-Catering
Quality Cottages, Cerbid, Solva, HAVERFORDWEST, Pembrokeshire SA62 6YE
Tel: 01348 837871
• e-mail: reserve@qualitycottages.co.uk
• website: www.qualitycottages.co.uk

Self-Catering
Ffynnon Ddofn, Llanon, Llanrhian, Near ST DAVIDS, Pembrokeshire.
Contact: Mrs B. Rees White, Brick House Farm, Burnham Road, Woodham Mortimer, Maldon, Essex CM9 6SR. Tel: 01245 224611
• e-mail: daisypops@madasafish.com
• website: www.ffynnonddofn.co.uk

•POWYS

Self-Catering
Lane Farm, Paincastle, BUILTH WELLS, Powys LD2 3JS
Tel: 01497 851 605
• e-mail: lanefarm@onetel.com
• website: www.lane-farm.co.uk

SCOTLAND

•ARGYLL & BUTE

Self-Catering
Appin House Lodges, APPIN, Argyll PA38 4BN
Tel: 01631 730207
• e-mail: denys@appinhouse.co.uk
• website: www.appinhouse.co.uk

Self-Catering
Blarghour Farm Cottages, Blarghour Farm, By Dalmally, INVERARAY, Argyll PA33 1BW
Tel: 01866 833246
• e-mail: blarghour@btconnect.com
• website: www.self-catering-argyll.co.uk

Hotel
Falls of Lora Hotel, Connel Ferry, By OBAN, Argyll PA37 1PB
Tel: 01631 710483
• e-mail: enquiries@fallsoflora.com
• website: www.fallsoflora.com

•DUMFRIES & GALLOWAY

Hotel
Corsewall Lighthouse Hotel, Kirkcolm, STRANRAER, Dumfries & Galloway DG9 0QG Tel: 01776 853220
• e-mail info@lighthousehotel.co.uk
• website: www.lighthousehotel.co.uk

•EDINBURGH & LOTHIANS

Self-Catering
Mrs C. M. Kilpatrick, Slipperfield House, WEST LINTON, Peeblesshire EH46 7AA
Tel: 01968 660401
• e-mail: cottages@slipperfield.com
• website: www.slipperfield.com

•HIGHLANDS

Self-Catering
Frank & Juliet Spencer-Nairn, Culligran Cottages, Struy, Near BEAULY, Inverness-shire IV4 7JX . Tel: 01463 761285
• e-mail: info@culligrancottages.co.uk
• website: www.culligrancottages.co.uk

FHG Guides

Caravan Park
A.J.Davis, Gruinard Bay Caravan Park,
LAIDE, Ross-shire IV22 2ND
Tel: 01445 731225
* e-mail: gruinard@ecosse.net
* website: www.gruinardbay.co.uk

•PERTH & KINROSS

Self-Catering
Atholl Cottage, Killiecrankie, PITLOCHRY,
Perthshire PH16 5LR
Contact: Mrs Joan Troup, Dalnasgadh,
Killiecrankie, Pitlochry, Perthshire PH16 5LN
Tel: 01796 470017
* e-mail: info@athollcottage.co.uk
* website: www.athollcottage.co.uk

•ORKNEY

Caravan & Camping
Point of Ness, STROMNESS, Orkney
Tel: 01856 873535
* e-mail: leisureculture@orkney.gov.uk
* websites: www.orkney.gov.uk
           www.hostelsorkney.co.uk

NORTHERN IRELAND

Caravan Park
Six Mile Water Carvan Park, Lough
Road, ANTRIM BT41 4DG
Tel: 028 9446 4963
* e-mail: sixmilewater@antrim.gov.uk
* website: www.antrim.gov.uk/caravanpark

INTERNET & Wi-Fi Access

•OXFORDSHIRE

DIDCOT • *B&B*

Middle Fell B&B, Moreton Road, Aston Upthorpe, Didcot OX11 9ER
Tel: 01235 850207 or 07833 920678
e-mail: middlefell@ic24.net
website: www.middlefell.co.uk
Wi-Fi connection in every room free of charge.

Accommodation Standards: Star Grading Scheme

The AA, VisitBritain, VisitScotland, and the VisitWales now use a single method of assessing and rating serviced accommodation. Irrespective of which organisation inspects an establishment the rating awarded will be the same, using a common set of standards, giving a clear guide of what to expect.   They have full details of the grading system on their websites.

 www.enjoyEngland.com

 www.visitScotland.com

 www.visitWales.com

www.theaa.com

Using a scale of 1-5 stars the objective quality ratings give a clear indication of accommodation standard, cleanliness, ambience, hospitality, service and food.

This shows the full range of standards suitable for every budget and preference, and allows visitors to distinguish between the quality of accommodation and facilities on offer in different establishments.
All types of board and self-catering accommodation are covered, including hotels, B&Bs, holiday parks, campus accommodation, hostels, caravans and camping, and boats.

Gold and Silver awards are given to Hotels and Guest Accommodation that provide exceptional quality, especially in service and hospitality.

The more stars, the higher level of quality

★
acceptable quality; simple, practical, no frills

★★
good quality, well presented and well run

★★★
very good level of quality and comfort

★★★★
excellent standard throughout

★★★★★
exceptional quality, with a degree of luxury

National Accessible Scheme Logos for mobility impaired and older people

If you have particular mobility impairment. look out for the National Accessible Scheme. You can be confident of finding accommodation or attractions that meet your needs by looking for the following symbols.

 Older and less mobile guests
If you have sufficient mobility to climb a flight of steps but would benefit from fixtures and fittings to aid balance.

 Part-time wheelchair users
You have restricted walking ability or may need to use a wheelchair some of the time and can negotiate a maximum of 3 steps.

 Independent wheelchair users
You are a wheelchair user and travel independently. Similar to the international logo for independent wheelchair users.

 Assisted wheelchair users
You're a wheelchair user and travel with a friend or family member who helps you with everyday tasks.

BEKONSCOT MODEL VILLAGE & RAILWAY
Warwick Road, Beaconsfield,
Buckinghamshire HP9 2PL
Tel: 01494 672919
e-mail: info@bekonscot.co.uk
www.bekonscot.co.uk

READERS' OFFER 2013

*One child FREE when accompanied by two
full-paying adults. Valid February to October 2013*

NOT TO BE USED IN CONJUNCTION WITH ANY OTHER OFFER

NENE VALLEY RAILWAY
Wansford Station, Stibbington,
Peterborough, Cambs PE8 6LR
Tel: 01780 784444
e-mail: nvrorg@nvr.org.uk
www.nvr.org.uk

READERS' OFFER 2013

One child FREE with each full paying adult.
Valid Jan. to end Oct. 2013 (excludes galas and pre-ticketed events)

NOT TO BE USED IN CONJUNCTION WITH ANY OTHER OFFER

TAMAR VALLEY DONKEY PARK
St Ann's Chapel, Gunnislake,
Cornwall PL18 9HW
Tel: 01822 834072
e-mail: info@donkeypark.com
www.donkeypark.com

READERS' OFFER 2013

*£1 OFF per person, up to 6 persons
Valid from Easter until end October 2013*

NOT TO BE USED IN CONJUNCTION WITH ANY OTHER OFFER

LAPPA VALLEY RAILWAY
Benny Halt, St Newlyn East,
Newquay, Cornwall TR8 5LX
Tel: 0844 4535543
e-mail: info@lappavalley.co.uk
www.lappavalley.co.uk

READERS' OFFER 2013

*£1 per person OFF up to a maximum of £4. Valid Easter
to end October 2013 (not on Family Saver tickets)*

NOT TO BE USED IN CONJUNCTION WITH ANY OTHER OFFER

Be a giant in a magical miniature world of make-believe depicting rural England in the 1930s. "A little piece of history that is forever England."

Open: 10am-5pm daily mid February to end October.

Directions: Junction 16 M25, Junction 2 M40.

FHG GUIDES, ABBEY MILL BUSINESS CENTRE, PAISLEY PA1 1TJ • www.holidayguides.com

Take a trip back in time on the delightful Nene Valley Railway with its heritage steam and diesel locomotives, There is a 7½ mile ride from Wansford to Peterborough via Yarwell, with shop, museum and excellent cafe at Wansford Station (free parking).

Open: please phone or see website for details.

Directions: situated 4 miles north of Peterborough on the A1

FHG GUIDES, ABBEY MILL BUSINESS CENTRE, PAISLEY PA1 1TJ • www.holidayguides.com

Cornwall's only Donkey Sanctuary set in 14 acres overlooking the beautiful Tamar Valley. Donkey grooming, goat hill, children's playgrounds, cafe and picnic area. All-weather play barn. Well behaved dogs on leads welcome.

Open: Easter to end Oct: daily 10am to 5pm. Nov to March: weekends and all school holidays 10.30am to 4.30pm

Directions: just off A390 between Callington and Gunnislake at St Ann's Chapel.

FHG GUIDES, ABBEY MILL BUSINESS CENTRE, PAISLEY PA1 1TJ • www.holidayguides.com

Three miniature railways, plus leisure park with canoes, crazy golf, large children's play area with fort, brickpath maze, wooded walks (all inclusive). Dogs welcome (50p).

Open: Easter to end October

Directions: follow brown tourist signs from A30 and A3075

FHG GUIDES, ABBEY MILL BUSINESS CENTRE, PAISLEY PA1 1TJ • www.holidayguides.com

THE BEACON
West Strand, Whitehaven,
Cumbria CA28 7LY
Tel: 01946 592302 • Fax: 01946 598150
e-mail: thebeacon@copelandbc.gov.uk
www.thebeacon-whitehaven.co.uk

*One FREE adult/concesssion when accompanied by one full paying
adult/concession. Under 16s free. Valid from Oct 2012 to end 2013.
Not valid for special events. Day tickets only.*

NOT TO BE USED IN CONJUNCTION WITH ANY OTHER OFFER

DEVONSHIRE COLLECTION OF PERIOD COSTUME
Totnes Fashion & Textiles Museum,
Bogan House, 43 High Street,
Totnes, Devon TQ9 5NP
Tel: 01803 862857 • www.devonmuseums.net

*FREE child with a paying adult with voucher
Valid from Spring Bank Holiday to end of Sept 2013*

NOT TO BE USED IN CONJUNCTION WITH ANY OTHER OFFER

WOODLANDS FAMILY THEME PARK
Blackawton, Dartmouth,
Devon TQ9 7DQ
Tel: 01803 712598 • Fax: 01803 712680
e-mail: fun@woodlandspark.com
www.woodlandspark.com

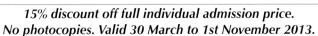

*15% discount off full individual admission price.
No photocopies. Valid 30 March to 1st November 2013.*

NOT TO BE USED IN CONJUNCTION WITH ANY OTHER OFFER

THE MILKY WAY ADVENTURE PARK
The Milky Way, Clovelly,
Bideford, Devon EX39 5RY
Tel: 01237 431255
e-mail: info@themilkyway.co.uk
www.themilkyway.co.uk

*10% discount on entrance charge.
Valid Easter to end October (not August).*

NOT TO BE USED IN CONJUNCTION WITH ANY OTHER OFFER

The Beacon is the Copeland area's interactive museum, tracing the area's rich history, from as far back as prehistoric times to the modern day. Enjoy panoramic views of the Georgian town and harbour from the 4th floor viewing gallery. Art gallery, gift shop, restaurant. Fully accessible.

Open: open all year (excl. 24-26 Dec) Tues-Sun, plus Monday Bank Holidays. Please contact before visit to check.

Directions: enter Whitehaven from north or south on A595. Follow the town centre and brown museum signs; located on harbourside.

FHG GUIDES, ABBEY MILL BUSINESS CENTRE, PAISLEY PA1 1TJ • www.holidayguides.com

---

Themed exhibition, changed annually, based in a Tudor house. Collection contains items of dress for women, men and children from 17th century to 1990s, from high fashion to everyday wear.

Open: Open from 22 May to end September. 11am to 5pm Tuesday to Friday.

Directions: centre of town, opposite Market Square. Mini bus up High Street stops outside.

FHG GUIDES, ABBEY MILL BUSINESS CENTRE, PAISLEY PA1 1TJ • www.holidayguides.com

---

A wide variety of rides, plus zoo and farm, makes a fantastic day out for all ages. Awesome indoor adventure centres, ball blasting arenas, mirror maze and soft play ensures wet days are fun. 16 family rides including white knuckle Swing Ship, electrifying Watercoasters, terrifying Toboggan Run, Superb Falconry Centre, Zoo Farm, tractor ride, weird and wonderful creatures. An all-weather attraction.

Open: 23 March to 3 November 2013 open daily 9.30am. In winter open weekends and local school holidays.

Directions: 5 miles from Dartmouth on A3122. Follow brown tourist signs from A38.

FHG GUIDES, ABBEY MILL BUSINESS CENTRE, PAISLEY PA1 1TJ • www.holidayguides.com

---

The day in the country that's out of this world! With 5 major rides and loads of great live shows.
See Merlin from 'Britain's Got Talent' 5 days a week. All rides and shows included in entrance fee.

Open: daily Easter to October. Please call or check online for full details.

Directions: on the main A39 one mile from Clovelly.

FHG GUIDES, ABBEY MILL BUSINESS CENTRE, PAISLEY PA1 1TJ • www.holidayguides.com

DORSET HEAVY HORSE FARM PARK

Edmondsham Road,
Near Verwood,
Dorset BH21 5RJ
Tel: 01202 824040
www.dorset-heavy-horse-centre.co.uk

READERS'
OFFER
2013

£1 off adult ticket. One voucher per person.
Not valid with any other offer or family ticket/concessions

NOT TO BE USED IN CONJUNCTION WITH ANY OTHER OFFER

KILLHOPE - THE NORTH OF ENGLAND LEAD MINING MUSEUM

Near Cowshill, Upper Weardale,
Co Durham DL13 1AR
Tel: 01388 537505 • Fax: 01388 537617
e-mail: info@killhope.org.uk
www.killhope.org.uk

READERS'
OFFER
2013

2-4-1 (cheapest free) or Like-4-Like
Valid April - October 2013

NOT TO BE USED IN CONJUNCTION WITH ANY OTHER OFFER

TWEDDLE CHILDREN'S ANIMAL FARM

Fillpoke Lane, Blackhall Colliery,
Co. Durham TS27 4BT
Tel: 0191 586 3311
e-mail: info@tweddlefarm.co.uk
www.tweddlefarm.co.uk

READERS'
OFFER
2013

FREE bag of animal food to every paying customer.
Valid until end 2013

NOT TO BE USED IN CONJUNCTION WITH ANY OTHER OFFER

BARLEYLANDS FARM & CRAFT VILLAGE

Barleylands Road, Billericay,
Essex CM11 2UD
Tel: 01268 290223 • Fax: 01268 290222
e-mail: info@barleylands.co.uk
www.barleylands.co.uk

READERS'
OFFER
2013

FREE entry for one child with each full paying adult. Valid
during 2013 - not with any other offer or on special events days.

NOT TO BE USED IN CONJUNCTION WITH ANY OTHER OFFER

Entertainment for all ages: fascinating daily shows, FREE wagon and tractor rides, straw fun barn, go-kart arena, gypsy wagons and Romany talks, blacksmith's workshop. Drive a real tractor, pony rides, 'hands-on' activities with the farm animals, over 20 rescued heavy horses. Lots undercover; cafe and gift shop + much more!

Open: 10am to 5pm Easter to end October.

Directions: On the Edmondsham Road, approx. 1½ miles from Verwood. Within easy reach of Bournemouth, Poole, Southampton, Ringwood and surrounding areas.

FHG GUIDES, ABBEY MILL BUSINESS CENTRE, PAISLEY PA1 1TJ • www.holidayguides.com

Killhope is a multi-award winning Victorian Lead Mining Museum, offering a grand day out. Accompany a guide on a mine tour. Our enthusiastic team ensure you have a day to remember, finding minerals, and working as a washerboy. Woodland trails, exhibitions, Killhope shop and cafe complete a great day out.

Open: April-October 10.30am-5pm

Directions: midway between Alston and Stanhope on A689

FHG GUIDES, ABBEY MILL BUSINESS CENTRE, PAISLEY PA1 1TJ • www.holidayguides.com

Children's farm and petting centre. Lots of hands on with bottle feeding events and bunny cuddling etc. Indoor and outdoor play areas, indoor and outdoor go-kart tracks, crazy golf, gift shop, tea room and lots more.

Open: March to Oct: 10am-5pm daily; Nov to Feb 10am to 4pm daily. Closed Christmas, Boxing Day and New Year's Day.

Directions: A181 from A19, head towards coast; signposted from there.

FHG GUIDES, ABBEY MILL BUSINESS CENTRE, PAISLEY PA1 1TJ • www.holidayguides.com

Set in over 700 acres of unspoilt Essex countryside, this former working farm is one of the county's most popular tourist attractions. The spectacular craft village and educational farm provide the perfect setting for a great day out.

Open: 7 days a week. March to October 10am-5pm; November to February 10am-4pm.

Directions: follow brown tourist signs from A127 and A12.

FHG GUIDES, ABBEY MILL BUSINESS CENTRE, PAISLEY PA1 1TJ • www.holidayguides.com

CIDER MUSEUM & KING OFFA DISTILLERY

21 Ryelands Street, Hereford,
Herefordshire HR4 0LW
Tel: 01432 354207
e-mail: enquiries@cidermuseum.co.uk
www.cidermuseum.co.uk

READERS' OFFER 2013

TWO for the price of ONE admission
Valid to end December 2013

NOT TO BE USED IN CONJUNCTION WITH ANY OTHER OFFER

SHEPRETH WILDLIFE PARK

Station Road, Shepreth,
Near Royston, Herts SG8 6PZ
Tel: 01763 262226
e-mail: office@sheprethwildlifepark.co.uk
www.sheprethwildlifepark.co.uk

READERS' OFFER 2013

FREE child with paying adult. Valid until 31/12/013
(excluding weekends and school holidays).

NOT TO BE USED IN CONJUNCTION WITH ANY OTHER OFFER

THE HELICOPTER MUSEUM

The Heliport, Locking Moor Road,
Weston-Super-Mare BS24 8PP
Tel: 01934 635227
e-mail: helimuseum@btconnect.com
www.helicoptermuseum.co.uk

READERS' OFFER 2013

One child FREE with two full-paying adults
Valid from April to December 2013

NOT TO BE USED IN CONJUNCTION WITH ANY OTHER OFFER

WEDGWOOD VISITOR CENTRE

Wedgwood Drive, Barlaston,
Stoke-on-Trent, Staffordshire ST12 9ER
Tel: 01782 282986 • Fax: 01782 223063
e-mail: bookings@wwrd.com
www.wedgwoodvisitorcentre.com

READERS' OFFER 2013

TWO for ONE offer on admission to Visitor Centre
(cheapest ticket free). Valid until end December 2013

NOT TO BE USED IN CONJUNCTION WITH ANY OTHER OFFER

Learn how traditional cider and perry was made, how the fruit was harvested, milled, pressed and bottled. Walk through original champagne cider cellars, and view 18th century lead crystal cider glasses.

Open:
April to Oct: 10am-5pm Mon-Sat.
Nov to March: 11am-3pm Mon-Sat.

Directions: off A438 Hereford to Brecon road, near Sainsbury's supermarket.

FHG GUIDES, ABBEY MILL BUSINESS CENTRE, PAISLEY PA1 1TJ • www.holidayguides.com

Wildlife park with a variety of species including tigers, mountain lions, meerkats, monkeys and otters. Indoor attractions include Waterworld, Bug City and Ringo's Playbarn.

Open: daily 10am-6pm (until dusk Winter/Spring). November-February closed Tuesday and Wednesday.

Directions: signposted off A10 between Royston and Cambridge. Two minutes from Shepreth rail station on Cambridge - London Kings X line.

FHG GUIDES, ABBEY MILL BUSINESS CENTRE, PAISLEY PA1 1TJ • www.holidayguides.com

The world's largest helicopter collection - over 70 exhibits, includes two royal helicopters, Russian Gunship and Vietnam veterans plus many award-winning exhibits. Cafe, shop. Flights.

PETS MUST BE KEPT UNDER CONTROL

Open: Wednesday to Sunday 10am to 5.30pm. Daily during school Easter and Summer holidays and Bank Holiday Mondays. November to March: 10am to 4.30pm

Directions: Junction 21 off M5 then follow the propellor signs.

FHG GUIDES, ABBEY MILL BUSINESS CENTRE, PAISLEY PA1 1TJ • www.holidayguides.com

The Wedgwood Factory, Visitor Centre and Museum is set in 260 acres of lush parkland. Enjoy a fascinating tour of the ceramic workshops and museum, guided factory tours, and the opportunity to make your own piece of Wedgwood at the home of Britain's greatest ceramic company.

Open: weekdays 10am-5pm weekends 10am-4pm

Directions: from M1 follow A50 west; from M6 follow A34, then brown tourist signs.

FHG GUIDES, ABBEY MILL BUSINESS CENTRE, PAISLEY PA1 1TJ • www.holidayguides.com

FHG
K·U·P·E·R·A·R·D
**READERS'
OFFER
2013**

FALCONRY UK BIRDS OF PREY CENTRE
Sion Hill Hall, Kirby Wiske
Near Thirsk, North Yorkshire YO7 4EU
Tel: 01845 587522
e-mail: mail@falconrycentre.co.uk
www.falconrycentre.co.uk

*TWO for ONE on admission to Centre. Cheapest ticket
free with voucher. Valid 1st March to 31st October.*

NOT TO BE USED IN CONJUNCTION WITH ANY OTHER OFFER

FHG
K·U·P·E·R·A·R·D
**READERS'
OFFER
2013**

MUSEUM OF RAIL TRAVEL
Ingrow Railway Centre, Near Keighley,
West Yorkshire BD21 5AX
Tel: 01535 680425
e-mail: admin@vintagecarriagestrust.org
www.vintagecarriagestrust.org

"ONE for ONE" free admission
Valid during 2013 except during special events (ring to check)

NOT TO BE USED IN CONJUNCTION WITH ANY OTHER OFFER

FHG
K·U·P·E·R·A·R·D
**READERS'
OFFER
2013**

RHEILFFORDD TALYLLYN RAILWAY
Gorsaf Wharf Station, Tywyn,
Gwynedd LL36 9EY
Tel: 01654 710472
e-mail: enquiries@talyllyn.co.uk
www.talyllyn.co.uk

20% OFF ticket price of full adult round trip
Not valid on special/excursion trains or Christmas services

NOT TO BE USED IN CONJUNCTION WITH ANY OTHER OFFER

FHG
K·U·P·E·R·A·R·D
**READERS'
OFFER
2013**

INIGO JONES SLATEWORKS
Groeslon, Caernarfon,
Gwynedd LL54 7UE
Tel: 01286 830242
e-mail: slate@inigojones.co.uk
www.inigojones.co.uk

TWO for the price of ONE on self-guided tour.
Valid during 2013

NOT TO BE USED IN CONJUNCTION WITH ANY OTHER OFFER

*Birds of prey centre with over
70 birds including owls, hawks,
falcons, kites, vultures and eagles.
3 flying displays daily.
When possible public welcome to
handle birds after each display.
No dogs allowed.*

Open: 1st March to 31st October
10.30am to 5pm. Flying displays
11.30am, 1.30pm and 3.30pm daily
(weather permitting).

Directions: on the A167 between
Northallerton and the Ripon turn off.
Follow brown tourist signs.

FHG GUIDES, ABBEY MILL BUSINESS CENTRE, PAISLEY PA1 1TJ • www.holidayguides.com

*A fascinating display of railway
carriages and a wide range of railway
items telling the story of rail travel
over the years.*

ALL PETS MUST BE KEPT ON LEADS

Open: daily 11am to 4pm

Directions: approximately one mile
from Keighley on A629 Halifax road.
Follow brown tourist signs

FHG GUIDES, ABBEY MILL BUSINESS CENTRE, PAISLEY PA1 1TJ • www.holidayguides.com

*The Talyllyn Railway is a historic
narrow-gauge steam railway running
through the beautiful mid-Wales
countryside, from Tywyn on the
coast to the delightful Dolgoch Falls
and wooded Nant Gwernol.*

Open: daily from Easter to October
and at other times of the year. See
website for details of timetables.

Directions: on the A493 on the
Aberdyfi side of Tywyn, 300 yards
from Tywyn mainline rail station and
bus stops.

FHG GUIDES, ABBEY MILL BUSINESS CENTRE, PAISLEY PA1 1TJ • www.holidayguides.com

*A unique, thriving, fully operational
slateworks. Enter the workshops for
a fascinating and inspiring insight
into an ongoing era of techniques
and expertise. Self-guided tours
including Lettercutting and
Calligraphy Exhibitions.*

Open: seven days a week 9am-
5pm. Closed Christmas/Boxing/New
Year's days

Directions: main A487 6 miles south
of Caernarfon going towards
Porthmadog.

FHG GUIDES, ABBEY MILL BUSINESS CENTRE, PAISLEY PA1 1TJ • www.holidayguides.com

GWILI RAILWAY
The Railway Station,
Bronwydd Arms,
Carmarthenshire SA33 6HT
Tel: 01267 238213
www.gwili-railway.co.uk

**READERS'
OFFER
2013**

*TWO FOR ONE (lowest price ticket free). Valid March-Oct 2013
except Thomas or "Special" events and/or Christmas*

NOT TO BE USED IN CONJUNCTION WITH ANY OTHER OFFER

THE GRASSIC GIBBON CENTRE
Arbuthnott, Laurencekirk,
Aberdeenshire AB30 1PB
Tel: 01561 361668
e-mail: lgginfo@grassicgibbon.com
www.grassicgibbon.com

**READERS'
OFFER
2013**

*TWO for the price of ONE entry to exhibition (based
on full adult rate only). Valid during 2013 (not groups)*

NOT TO BE USED IN CONJUNCTION WITH ANY OTHER OFFER

BO'NESS & KINNEIL RAILWAY
Bo'ness Station, Union Street,
Bo'ness, West Lothian EH51 9AQ
Tel: 01506 822298
e-mail: enquiries.railway@srps.org.uk
www.bkrailway.com

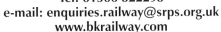

**READERS'
OFFER
2013**

*FREE child train fare with one paying adult/concession.
Valid April-Oct 2013. Not Premier Fare events*

NOT TO BE USED IN CONJUNCTION WITH ANY OTHER OFFER

SCOTTISH DEER CENTRE
Cupar,
Fife KY15 4NQ
Tel: 01337 810391
e-mail: info@tsdc.co.uk
www.tsdc.co.uk

**READERS'
OFFER
2013**

*One child FREE with one full paying adult on
production of voucher. Not valid during December.*

NOT TO BE USED IN CONJUNCTION WITH ANY OTHER OFFER

During operating days we provide a trip back in time with a round trip on a steam-hauled locomotive in the scenic Gwili valley.
Pay once and ride all day.
Check website or phone for timetables.

Open: check website or phone for information.

Directions: just off the A484, three miles north of Carmarthen.

FHG GUIDES, ABBEY MILL BUSINESS CENTRE, PAISLEY PA1 1TJ • www.holidayguides.com

---

Visitor Centre dedicated to the much-loved Scottish writer Lewis Grassic Gibbon. Exhibition, cafe, gift shop. Outdoor children's play area. Disabled access throughout.

Open: daily March to October 10am to 4.30pm. Groups by appointment including evenings.

Directions: on the B967, accessible and signposted from both A90 and A92.

FHG GUIDES, ABBEY MILL BUSINESS CENTRE, PAISLEY PA1 1TJ • www.holidayguides.com

---

Steam and heritage diesel passenger trains from Bo'ness to Manuel.
Explore the history of Scotland's railways in the Museum of Scottish Railways. Coffee shop and souvenir shop.

Open: weekends April to October, most days in July and August.
See website for dates and timetables.

Directions: in the town of Bo'ness. Leave M9 at Junction 3 or 5, then follow brown tourist signs.

FHG GUIDES, ABBEY MILL BUSINESS CENTRE, PAISLEY PA1 1TJ • www.holidayguides.com

---

55-acre park with 14 species of deer from around the world. Guided tours, trailer rides, treetop walkway, children's adventure playground and picnic area. Other animals include wolves, foxes, otters and a bird of prey centre.

Open: 10am to 5pm daily except Christmas Day and New Year's Day.

Directions: A91 south of Cupar. Take J9 M90 from the north, J8 from the south.

FHG GUIDES, ABBEY MILL BUSINESS CENTRE, PAISLEY PA1 1TJ • www.holidayguides.com

Index of Towns and Counties

Other FHG Titles

FHG Guides Ltd have been publishing an attractive range of holiday accommodation guides for 65 years. For all kinds of holiday opportunities, they make useful gifts at any time of year.

The Original **Pets Welcome!** £9.99
The bestselling guide to holidays for pets and their owners
Quality properties where pets are warmly welcomed
Including Pet-Friendly Pubs & Dog Friendly Walks
60th edition

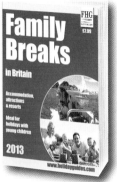

750 Bed & Breakfasts £9.99
in Britain
For holidaymakers
and business travellers
Overnight stops and Short Breaks

Family Breaks £7.99
in Britain
• Accommodation, attractions and resorts
• Ideal for holidays with young children

The Golf Guide £12.99
Where to Play, Where to Stay
• Details of 3000 Clubs and Courses
  in Britain and Ireland
• Location, facilities, statistics
• Plus accommodation

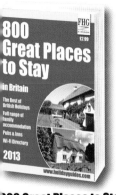

800 Great Places to Stay £7.99
in Britain
The Best of British Holidays
Full range of family accommodation

Self Catering Holidays £8.99
in Britain
• Cottages, farms, apartments and chalets
• Pet-Friendly accommodation

Short Break Holidays £8.99
in Britain
• Accommodation for holidays
  and weekends away

FHG
·K·U·P·E·R·A·R·D·

Our guides are available in most bookshops and larger newsagents but we will be happy to post you a copy direct if you have any difficulty.

POST FREE for addresses in the UK.

We will also post abroad but have to charge separately for post or freight.

☐ **The Original Pets Welcome!**

☐ **750 Bed & Breakfasts** in Britain

☐ **Family Breaks** in Britain

☐ **Short Break Holidays** in Britain

☐ **800 Great Places to Stay** in Britain

☐ **Self Catering Holidays** in Britain

☐ **Caravan & Camping Holidays** in Britain

☐ **The Golf Guide** Where to Play • Where to Stay in Britain & Ireland

To order: print this page, tick your choice above and send your order and payment to

FHG Guides Ltd. Abbey Mill Business Centre

Seedhill, Paisley, Scotland PA1 1TJ

TEL: 0141- 887 0428 • FAX: 0141- 889 7204

e-mail: admin@fhguides.co.uk

Deduct 10% for 2/3 titles or copies; 20% for 4 or more.

Send to: NAME ....

ADDRESS ....

....

....

POST CODE ....

I enclose Cheque/Postal Order for £ ....

SIGNATURE ....DATE ....

© FHG Guides Ltd, 2013
ISBN 978-1-85055-457-8

Typeset by FHG Guides Ltd, Paisley.
Printed and bound in China by Imago.

Distribution. Book Trade: ORCA Book Services, Stanley House,
3 Fleets Lane, Poole, Dorset BH15 3AJ
Tel: 01202 665432; Fax: 01202 666219
e-mail: mail@orcabookservices.co.uk

Published by FHG Guides Ltd., Abbey Mill Business Centre,
Seedhill, Paisley PA1 ITJ
Tel: 0141-887 0428; Fax: 0141-889 7204
e-mail: admin@fhguides.co.uk

Caravan & Camping Holidays in Britain is published by FHG Guides Ltd,
part of Kuperard Group.

Cover design: FHG Guides
Cover Pictures: Carnmoggas Holiday Park, St Austell, Cornwall (see p16)
                  Castaways Holiday Park, Bacton-on-Sea, Norfolk (see page 80)